Praise for Diana G. Blanco & *Smooth Baby Sleep*

"Diana Blanco has created a winner of a book for parents, babies and their pediatricians! This is a comprehensive guide to baby's sleep and 'just what the doctor ordered' for the parent who feels like they are at wit's end to get a good night's sleep for themself and their child. This book can be read straight through and used as a comprehensive tool for sleep information at different stages of a baby or child's life.

For those frazzled parents who want the '911 answers' Ms. Blanco has created this book such that those parents can go straight to the sections that apply to their problem and begin to utilize the techniques immediately. She gives parents a customized approach to helping baby develop good sleep habits, which not only serves them well in the formative years, but also sets the child up for healthy sleeping habits for a lifetime.

This is the most comprehensive and parent-friendly book I have seen to address this important topic of sleep."

> Melissa M. Brown, M.D.
> Board Certified Pediatrician & Life Coach
> Short Hills, NJ. USA

"Reading this book was like having a sleep consultant in my home, coaching me privately, as I helped my son sleep better. It is a must read for all new moms who want to teach their babies to develop healthy sleep habits but do not want to go through nights of crying it out."

> Alison Carlton
> Mother to Samuel, 11 months old
> New York City, NY. USA

"After 3 years co-sleeping with my daughter, I couldn't do it anymore. I was exhausted, and she was sleep deprived. Diana's plan worked like a charm. Whitney was so proud of herself during the process; she couldn't wait to tell everyone about her 'big-girl bed.' Within just a couple of weeks, she was sleeping in her bedroom all by herself, without crying and without waking up."

Alice Murray
Mother to Whitney, 3 years old
Sidney, AUSTRALIA

"I feel like a new woman! I have energy! I can get things done during the day, and most importantly, I can be a better mom to Cole and focus on things that are important, like playing and cooking. Working with Diana was the best money we've spent so far on anything baby related. Her advice is easy to follow, and her coaching style is very reassuring."

Amity S.
Mom to Cole, 10 months old
Brooklyn, NY, USA

"My husband and I followed Diana Blanco's sleep methods, and after just two weeks, we put an end to 15 months of struggling. My preemie twin daughters were for the first time sleeping 12 hours through the night and napping another 2 hours daily. At 22 months, we are still following Diana's teachings, and my daughters continue sleeping wonderfully."

Maria C., R.N.
Mom to Jazmine & Bella, 15 months old
Wayne, NJ, USA

"Angelina never had an issue going to sleep at night; her problem was that she would wake up 3-4 times during the night. At 11 months old, I decided to implement Diana's plan, I was prepared for a long night with tea, chocolate and a good movie to distract me; but I didn't need them. Angelina only woke up twice, and I was able to settle her very quickly. I was shocked! The next night, she only woke up once and fell asleep even faster. Ever since, she has been sleeping 11-12 hours straight and falls asleep more easily for her naps, as well."

Brooke B.
Mom to Angelina, 11 months old
Boston, MA, USA

"After meeting with Diana, my husband and I finally had a plan. We were prepared for a tough road ahead. On the first night, Nate still had 3 night wakings, but he was actually able to fall right back asleep without our help. By the second night, he was sleeping through the night, completely uninterrupted! We continued to be consistent, and within a few days, Nate was not only sleeping in his crib at night but also during nap times as well. We have been following the plan ever since, and currently, Nate sleeps about 11 and a half hours at night and takes 2 naps that are between an hour to an hour and a half long.

I am so happy that I contacted Diana. A good night's sleep has not only helped Nate become a happier, well-rested boy, but it has improved our whole family's life!"

Michal K.
Mom to Nathan, 14 months old preemie
New York, NY, USA

"This book has been a life saver to us. We used to take turns to sleep, struggle every night at bedtime, be in a terrible mood all the time, and not be able to function properly. We followed Diana's plan with our three children, and it worked amazingly. It took us a little over a month to get the three of them on the right track. The process was very peaceful, gentle, and very effective. Thanks for the gift of sleep!"

Thomas and Carrie Williams
Parents to Anthony, 6 months old; Brian,
2.5 years old; and Amanda, 4 years old
Vancouver Island, CANADA

"Diana Blanco changed my family's life. I used to spend 2 hours every night trying to get my 26 month-old daughter, Isabella, to fall asleep; and still, she wasn't getting enough sleep. She was always whining, cranky, unhappy and tired. Within 3 days of implementing Diana's plan, my daughter was sleeping 12 hours at night and napping for 2 hours every day. My daughter is happier and more alert during the day, and she enjoys going to bed every night. I wholeheartedly recommend Smooth Parenting's methods to every mom—because it works!"

Andreina Quijada de Ramirez
Mom to Isabella, 26 months old
Caracas, VENEZUELA

SMOOTH BABY SLEEP

6 Simple Steps to Gently Teach Your Baby to Sleep

Diana G. Blanco, M.B.A., C.P.Y.F.C
Certified Parenting and Family Coach. Child Sleep Expert.

Contact Diana G. Blanco at: www.SmoothParenting.com

For Information address: **Smooth Parenting**
646.450.660.5 | contact@smoothparenting.com
www.SmoothParenting.com | www.SmoothBabySleepBook.com

ISBN: 978-0-9835221-0-2
Cover design by Ariane Bibas, http://www.lucaria.com
Cover photograph copyright: © HaywireMedia - Fotolia.com

Safety Notice: About the Cover Photograph
The cover picture was chosen for its aesthetics and design. However, the baby is not placed in a safe sleeping position. Babies should always be placed to sleep on their backs, as explained in more detail in this book.

Limits of Liability and Disclaimer of Warranty
The purpose of this book is to educate and entertain. The advice, suggestions, and comments offered in this book, including any advice, techniques, and ideas on caring for your children and/or on parenting are undertaken at the reader's discretion and responsibility. Should the reader decided to follow all or part of the advice provided, the reader does so entirely at her own risk, and by voluntarily undertaking such risk, the client hereby releases the author, publisher and Smooth Parenting, from any and all claims, actions, damages, obligations, or liabilities caused, or alleged to be caused, directly or indirectly by the information in this book.
Some names and identifying characteristics of people in the book have been changed to protect the privacy of the individuals.

FIRST EDITION

*This book is dedicated with eternal love and gratitude
to my husband, Aser,
for his unwavering support and belief in me,
for helping me be a better mother and spouse,
and for his love and respect;*

*and to my daughters, Emma and Alba,
for inspiring me every day,
for giving me the courage to be my best self,
for their smiles and unconditional love,
and for choosing me to be their mother.*

I love you.

TABLE OF CONTENTS

PART V: COMMON & SPECIAL CIRCUMSTANCES

PART V: APPENDIX

GENDER IN THE BOOK

Due to the lack of a genderless pronoun in the English language to refer to boys and girls indistinctively, I will be alternating the use of 'he' and 'she' throughout the book, without it meaning any gender preference on my part. I believe that both boys and girls are equally wonderful and special and that they all have the potential to become great sleepers.

"It is never too late to be what you might have been."
                                    - GEORGE ELIOT

PART I:

INTRODUCTION

Chapter One

HOW TO READ THIS BOOK

My main goal with this book is to give you the tools that you need to solve your child's sleep problems and to empower you in your role as a parent. I would like to inspire you with this book to take a step back and believe in yourself and to trust your instincts. We have come to a point where parenting is an extremely polarizing topic, and sleep is at the top of the list of controversial issues. Many moms and dads are afraid or ashamed to speak up about their struggles and their approaches to parenting, sleep training, discipline, or breastfeeding. Nowadays, parents seem to be doomed if they are disciplinarians or if they free-range; if they breastfeed or if they bottle-feed; if they carry their babies or if they don't; if they are followers of Dr. Sears or if they are followers of Dr. Weissbluth... It seems like there's never a way to do things right. It's suffocating!

Know that whatever you decide to do, you'll always have critics. Do not let anyone bring you down and make you feel that you are not a good parent or that you are doing it wrong. I encourage you not to believe that you need to meet your friends', parents', or society's standards when it comes to parenting. **The only standards you need to meet are yours and your children's.**

I would also love to invite you to accept other parents' approaches to parenting (unless they are harming or abusing their

8

children), look at them with an open mind, and understand that, at the end of the day, **we all want what's best for our children.**

After reading almost every book out there on baby sleep, I realized that most of them shared the following same three flaws: (1) They are either too light in content so that they don't offer enough information, or they are too heavy so that exhausted and sleep deprived parents give up before finishing them; (2) They lack practical step by step guidelines; and (3) They argue that there is one sleep training method that is good for every child and every family.

Therefore, my promise to you is that in this book I will do the following:

- Make your sleep training process as easy, happy and smooth as possible;
- Share with you just the right amount of information so that you understand the basics of how baby sleep works, but not too much so that you get overwhelmed by it;
- Provide you with step-by-step guidelines to teach your baby to sleep; and
- Help you choose the best approach for your child and your family.

Even though I would love for you to read the whole book, as I truly believe I am sharing essential information with you, I understand that you might be at your wits' end, that you might not have the time to read everything, and that you wanted a solution yesterday. Therefore, here are some shortcuts that you might want to follow:

- If you want to know why I'm so interested in sleep, what makes me an expert, and my personal experience with sleep, read Chapter two - About the Author.

- If you want to understand how baby sleep works and why it is such an essential part of your child's development, delve into Part II – Baby Sleep Basics.
- If you want to jump right into the Smooth Baby Sleep Approach and start building your child's customized sleep plan, read Part III – Your Child's Customized Smooth Baby Sleep Plan. The first section – Design - will walk you step by step through how to build your child's plan. The second section – Implementation – will explain you how to put the plan that you have designed into practice, and actually start helping your child become a better sleeper.
- If have a premature child, have multiples (twins, triplets, and more), have a child on the autistic spectrum, you will also want to read Chapter ten – Special Considerations.
- If you want to know my answer to common questions such as what to do about "frequent night wakings," "sleep training and breastfeeding," "travel and sleep," "daylight savings" and more, go to Chapter nine – Common Sleep Challenges & Circumstances.

As you go along, you will be referred to the "Appendix" of the book, where you will find all the templates you need to build your child's customized sleep plan and additional resources. If you prefer to download those templates instead of writing in the book, you can go to the website www.SmoothBabySleepBook.com. Once there, click on the "Templates & Trackers" section and introduce the code SBSBOOK.

In this website, you will not only be able to download the templates, cheat sheets, and workbooks that I mentioned and covered throughout the book, but you'll also find additional resources and gifts. These resources were designed for you, the reader of this book. Please do not share them with anyone who hasn't read the book, as it all goes together.

The book is filled with case studies and sample stories—some from the many families who have followed this method to successfully sleep train their children and some from my personal experience as a mother of twins, as a friend, and as a daughter. Remember as you go over them, that your child will not fit any of the specific profiles described in those stories. Your child has his own personality, temperament, biological cycles, and circumstances, and all those elements will come into play during his sleep training process. Your goal, as a parent, is to find the best way to help him develop positive sleep associations and good sleep habits; this book will help you with that. **Believe in yourself and in your child! Together, you can do it!**

Chapter Two

ABOUT THE AUTHOR

My Story

I was born in Spain, the oldest of almost 30 cousins, so I have always been around babies and toddlers. I have always loved children. I am passionate about children development and child psychology, about health and family issues, and about parenting and how it can impact a child's emotional, psychological, and physical growth.

Even though I had read all the books, websites, articles, and magazines that came near me on those topics; even though I loved helping parents and caring for children; and even though deep inside I knew I had a gift to share and that this was my calling; I didn't think that it could ever be my professional career. So, I took the "conventional" path, and I graduated with my Bachelor in Business from the University of Wales and my Master in Business from New York University. I then proceeded to work in Strategy and Marketing for over 10 years. My last several jobs were highly paid, competitive, and coveted positions at Fortune 500 companies.

I continued reading and learning about all those topics that I loved, but I never thought I would have the courage to leave my successful management career. I desperately longed to do what I loved doing, which was helping parents have a smoother, easier and happier parenting experience and, therefore, helping children have the childhood and upbringing they deserved and grow up to be the wonderful, accomplished, happy, balanced, independent individuals they were meant to be from the start.

When my twin daughters were born 2 months premature, something shifted inside of me. One of the things that first came to my attention was that all my instincts in caring for my babies (even the premature ones) were right. Other moms were turning to me for advice. Doctors, nurses, and pediatric therapists would compliment my parenting skills and innate ability to understand children and meet their needs.

I know this "gift" has always been in me, but **somehow, I hid it** behind my business career. Finally, I decided it was time for me to follow my passion and to start helping parents in a bigger and better way. I quit my job in Corporate America; got certified as a youth, parenting, and family coach; became a member of the American Academy of Sleep Medicine; and launched Smooth Parenting.

Smooth Parenting is an infant and toddler sleep consultancy and parenting-coaching organization that helps families around the world. My goal is to provide parents with useful, direct, and practical advice to help them become the parents they have always wanted to be, connect with their children, eliminate unnecessary fights and struggles, and enjoy parenthood. I want parents to have a "Smooth Parenting Experience."

For more information about Smooth Parenting, about me, about how I work with families, and to read real families' stories, visit my website www.SmoothParenting.com. You will also be able to download an audio recording of one of my most praised classes.

Why am I so interested in baby sleep?

My interest in baby and toddler sleep started early on. I remember my parents always mentioning that I was a terrible sleeper when I was a baby and that I kept them up all night, crying and fussing, for weeks and months. My parents would try a different thing every night to get me to sleep: rocking, nursing, humming, swaddling, co-sleeping, car rides, stroller rides, and pretty much everything they could think of—except leaving me to cry myself to sleep (for which I'm extremely thankful). However, nothing worked. Apparently, it was impossible to get me to sleep. That went on for the first few years of my life.

At gatherings with my extended family, I would also hear many of my aunts describing the same struggle when trying to get my cousins to sleep. I wondered whether there was something in our family that made babies lack the ability to sleep.

As I grew older, I realized that many of my parent's friends with smaller children had the same challenges getting them to sleep. I started developing an interest in the subject from a very early age. I would also observe in detail how the parents with young children around me would treat sleep and what their approach to sleep training was. When my youngest brother, Adrian, was born, I was able to see firsthand how my parents dealt with his sleep and how it eventually became a problem as well. I read as many books as I could on the subject then, which weren't that many actually, and I would observe and analyze. I found several commonalities, patterns, and habits that contributed either positively or negatively to baby and children's sleep. I can honestly say that before I reached my teen years, I had a pretty good idea of how to identify a child's sleep problems based on many different factors (character, family dynamics, parenting approach, routines, age, etc.) and what the best approach to solve those problems might be, based on those factors.

As I grew up, had access to more books and the Internet, and was surrounded by more children, I continued educating myself on baby sleep (and many other parenting topics), and I continued analyzing every family around me.

I had the opportunity to test my method with many kids that I had the chance to babysit for. Even though, I do not have a magic wand that allows me to turn a situation around in one night, I was able to set the path for the parents to continue improving their child's sleep habits.

As an adult, I realized how much of an impact the sleep habits I developed when I was a child determined my own sleep habits as an adult. **I grew up a terrible sleeper, and to this day, I am still a bad sleeper**. Every day, I have to remind myself of the importance of sleep, and every day, I have to keep myself on track. I certainly wouldn't be in this situation had I been helped to develop healthy sleep habits from the start. **Children do not outgrow their sleep problems; they carry them around to adulthood**.

When I got pregnant with my twin daughters, I knew I didn't want to go through what my parents when through and make my daughters go through what I went through as a baby. However, I was a little intimidated by the task of raising twins. I had never worked with twins before. In fact, I hadn't ever even observed twins before. I didn't know anyone with twins, and I didn't know how well my approach to sleep would work in this situation.

When my daughters came home from the hospital, where they had spent the first weeks of their lives, my husband and I started following my sleep training approach. I must say that for first time parents of twins, we were sleeping quite well. At some point, though, we derailed a little bit from our habits. This was mainly because we were (at least I was) too concerned about their health and prematurity. I was a little too worried (without major reasons why) about losing them, so I would do things that didn't resonate with my approach to baby sleep coaching and that I would never recommend the families I work with should do.

My main pet peeves during the 2-3 weeks that my daughters' sleep habits got a little derailed were these: inconsistency and distraction. I was stressed trying to figure out whether I should go back to my corporate job. I had some arguments with my mother, who had come for a couple of weeks to help out. I was struggling with breastfeeding and pumping, and I wasn't completely focused on how my emotions were getting in the way of my daughters' sleep.

I must say the situation never got completely out of hand, but there were a couple of weeks when their sleep was not as good as it should've been. I wasn't following my own plan. As soon as I realized the problem, my husband and I sat down, figured out what we needed to do to turn the situation around, and got back to happy nights and days. Within a couple of days, my daughters were again the awesome sleepers that they had been up to that point. That experience proved to me how we, parents, have a major influence in our children's sleep habits and how we have it in our hands to turn any situation around.

Why did I write this book?

The information about baby sleep is confusing

There is so much conflicting information out there that many new parents feel completely overwhelmed by it to the point where it paralyzes them. Everyone tells you something different and contradictory about how to help your baby sleep, and the panorama does not improve when you resort to books. Every book gives different advice and criticized the other ones. Not even the medicine professionals agree on what the best approach to teach children how to sleep is.

Our sleep quality affects our parenting

Parenting can be stressful at times, especially when sleep issues arise. Sleep challenges are without a doubt the number one topic of conversation amongst new parents. Sleep deprivation affects the whole family, and it has long-lasting consequences. That coupled with the constant external and self-imposed guilt that many new parents (especially new moms) are surrounded by is a recipe for disaster.

My life purpose is to empower caring parents

I know firsthand the problems that having poor sleep habits can cause a person, and I know the struggle that parents and babies go through when they are sleep deprived. I wanted to give you, parents, a simple, easy-to-follow, customizable, and effective method to help your child to sleep. I am aware that not everyone can afford working with me one on one, but you still deserve to be helped in this process and feel empowered as parents again. Reading this book is the closest experience that you can have to working with me one on one. I'm thrilled to be sharing 'my method' with you, since I know it will transform your family life for the better.

Smooth Baby Sleep Works

Smooth Baby Sleep WORKS. I have worked with all sorts of families and situations, and I have successfully implemented the Smooth Baby Sleep approach. It has worked for…

- Brady, 21-month-old, autistic boy, who wasn't able to fall asleep in his own bed. He was disturbed in his sleep by the softest noise, light, and any kind of movement in the house.
- Jazmine and Bella, 15-month-old, premature twins, who didn't know how to fall asleep on their own, didn't nap, and woke up multiple times during the night.
- Cole, 10-month-old, breastfed boy, who couldn't self-soothe, needed to be nursed to fall sleep, woke up multiple times during the night to be nursed back to sleep again, and didn't nap consistently.
- Blake, 9-month-old boy, who couldn't fall asleep unless he was being rocked, woke consistently at 4:30 a.m. ready to start the day, and only catnapped during the day.
- Tamara, 28-month-old girl, who had been mistakenly diagnosed with ADHD. She would only sleep 8 hours at night, and her naptime and bedtime rituals had become an

almost 2 hour event. She had taken over her parents' bed, where she would sleep with her mom, and her dad slept on the floor by them.

- Jason and Simon, 4 and 2-year-old brothers, who had gotten used to sleeping by the TV in the living room, woke up to play at 2 a.m. every day, and would stay up for as long as 2 hours.
- Isabella, 23-month-old girl, who needed her mom to lay down with her every night for hours on end to fall asleep, only to wake up after a couple of hours and jump in to her parents' bed.
- Edward, 20-month-old boy, who woke up every 2 hours to nurse for a couple of minutes, co-slept, and couldn't nap unless in motion (stroller or car). Edward's mom, Laura, is a full-time, working outside of the home, single mom, with no family living nearby.

I could fill an entire book only with the stories of families that I've worked with and have successfully turned their children's sleep situation around. Each story is different and unique, but what remains the same is that because of my Smooth Baby Sleep Approach, they are all leading happier, more restful lives. I will be sharing with you some of these families' stories throughout the book so that you can find inspiration and encouragement from them. **If these parents could do it, you can do it too!**

Chapter Three

THE SMOOTH PARENTING APPROACH

*"The more people have studied different methods of bringing
up children, the more they have come to the conclusion that
what good mothers and fathers instinctively feel like doing
for their babies is the best after all."*

– BENJAMIN SPOCK, MD

Before we become parents, we see ourselves avoiding the mistakes we identified in other parents, balancing our professional and family lives, keeping our smiles and joy, being fantastic role models to our children, and knowing how to overcome all the challenges that might arise. Once we become parents, we realize that there is a reason why people say that parenting is the hardest "job" out there (if done well!). We sometimes find ourselves at our wits' end, not knowing what to do next. Others, we just go through the motions and see the days and weeks go by before our eyes.

Parenting should not be as hard as we think or we make it to be. Parenting should be smooth, full of heartwarming moments, and enjoyable. I'm not saying that it should always be fun, that it should come without challenges, and that it should be easy; I'm not saying that. What I'm saying is that we all can be the great parents we want to be, and that we can all have the Smooth Parenting Experience that we had always envisioned.

20

Sometimes, we need to...

- Take a step back and appreciate what we have.
- Acknowledge that we don't have all the answers.
- Be aware and mindful of how our own actions, feelings, expectations, and emotional baggage are influencing our children.
- Let go of the dream that there's such a thing as a super mom or super dad, who always gets it right from the very first try..
- Analyze what we are doing and improve it.
- Take the back seat and let our children teach us how they need to be parented and what it is that really need from us.
- Get support to solve the more challenging situations.

In any of these situations, we are taking action, and that is the first step to become the parent you want to be and have that smooth parenting experience. **You can be the parent you want to be! Yes, you can!**

This is what I believe when it comes to parenting:

- Every child is unique, special and should be treated as such.
- Parents should promote and support the physical, emotional, social, and intellectual development of their children from babyhood to adulthood.
- Parents must adapt their parenting approach to their child's individual needs, personality, and character.
- Children must know that they are unconditionally loved and that their parents will always be there for them.
- Children must feel happy, respected, valued, loved, acknowledged, safe, and protected in order to thrive and achieve their highest potential in life.
- The dignity and rights of children must be respected.

- Sleeping, eating, and exercising are basic needs for babies and children.
- Consistency and teamwork are key in order to be successful at parenting.
- Babies and children thrive when their lives are organized and when they know what's expected of them.
- An "structured routine" adapted to each family's individual circumstances is essential to create a chaos-free and stress-free home.
- There's always a reason/motivation/cause for children to cry, protest, misbehave, be aggressive, etc. In order to solve that behavior, parents need to discover it and find a solution. More often than not, our own expectations, actions, behavior, feelings and words are what are getting in the way of our children growing up to be who they are meant to be.
- It is important for parents to model appropriate behavior and to establish expectations as well as limits.
- Physical punishment or disciplining techniques are never the right way to go.

I apply each and every one of those principles to all areas of parenting, sleep included. My parenting techniques promote independence, self-esteem, self-assurance, self-awareness, consciousness, mindfulness, open communication, love, trust, empowerment, and self-improvement.

PART II:

BABY SLEEP BASICS

Chapter Four

WHY SLEEP MATTERS

"Your life is a reflection of how you sleep, and how you sleep is a reflection of your life."

- DR. PELAYO,
MD, PEDIATRIC NEUROLOGIST

Sleep is important, for it affects everything and everyone. Having worked with hundreds of families and being the mom of two premature babies, I know what a difference sleep makes for their development, growth, and improvement. Sleep profoundly affects the quality of our well-being in a manner that is unrivaled by almost any other factor. Sleep deprivation affects our parenting style; our relationship with our partner, family, and friends; our work; our health; and our outlook on life.

This knowledge about "why" it is so important to give your baby the gift of excellent sleep habits will act as reinforcement during any periods of doubt that you have as you move through the process of implementing your Smooth Baby Sleep Plan. You are responsible for your children's sleep habits, so it is important to start healthy ones early. It is much easier to instill healthy habits than it is correcting unhealthy ones. Children do not "outgrow" sleep problems; they must be solved during childhood, or they will be carried over to adulthood. Therefore, I advise you to infuse the importance of sleep from the start, with daily attention to it.

Lack of adequate sleep can affect judgment, mood and the ability to learn and retain information, and it may increase the risk of accidents and injury in the short term. In the long term, chronic sleep deprivation may lead to a host of health problems including obesity, diabetes, cardiovascular disease, and even early mortality. The negative effects of sleep deprivation are even more severe in children.

I don't share this with you to scare or alarm you but to make you aware of what the signs are and what the consequences could be, when sleep deprivation takes place in early childhood. **The good news is that this is a fixable problem. It will require discipline, teamwork, consistency, and positivity on your part,** and it will be difficult for your child. However, in the long run, all the effort will pay off.

Effect on Parents

Depression, Hopelessness, Ill-fated Parenting and Baby at Risk

Almost all parents suffer from sleep deprivation during the first months of their baby's life. Sleep deprivation leaves us feeling disorientated, confused, hopeless, frustrated, and irritable—all of which lead to a higher risk of depression. As a result of depression, parents interact less with their baby, have difficulty attaching and bonding to their baby, can't properly read their baby's cues and respond to them accordingly, and are less responsive to their baby's needs. Therefore, sleep deprivation hampers a mother's (and father's) ability to care for her baby and to be the parent that she's always dreamed she'd be.

When you are sleep deprived, you may be irritated with your baby, blaming her for your lack of sleep. Even though this might not even be crossing your mind right now, you might end up putting your baby at risk. On the extreme side, sleep deprivation and postpartum depression can lead to more serious problems of neglect, abuse, psychosis, or suicidal thoughts. These potential severe consequences *cannot* be ignored.

Some parents are pushed too far by sleep deprivation and admit to shaking or smacking their babies to make them stop crying and start sleeping. Several studies suggest that a baby is more likely to suffer from Shaken Baby Syndrome by parents who suffer from postpartum depression. It only takes a couple of seconds to damage your baby for life or even cause terminal damage.

Don't Shake Your Baby!

SBS/AHT (Shaken Baby Syndrome/Abusive Head Trauma) is a term used to describe the constellation of signs and symptoms resulting from violent shaking or the shaking and impacting of the head of an infant or small child. SBS is a form of physical child abuse that occurs when someone violently shakes an infant or small child, creating a whiplash-type motion that causes acceleration-deceleration injuries.

SBS is often fatal (mortality rate 15% to 38%) and can cause severe brain damage, resulting in lifelong disabilities (blindness, cerebral palsy, cognitive impairments, etc.).

Do not EVER shake your baby!

Self-Worth & Happiness

There is nothing better than a good night's sleep to make you feel better. Getting consistent, restful sleep is strongly correlated to being happy and productive and feeling healthy, both mentally and emotionally. Sleep has a significant effect on a person's well-being; persistent poor sleep can cause people to feel unplugged with what's going on in their lives. Parents who don't get enough sleep commonly worry that they are not spending enough time with their children or engaging with them enough because of fatigue and fogginess. There's no doubt about it, sleep definitely has an effect on our emotional well-being.

I strongly believe that happy parents equal happy babies, and the opposite is also true. Therefore, if you want yourself and your child to be happy, I encourage you to listen to Gretchen Rubin, author of *The Happiness Project,* when she says, "*One Easy Key to Happiness: Get More Sleep.*"

Relationship & Intimacy Problems

Sleep problems cause increased irritability, frustration, and mood swings, which intensify problems and disagreements with your partner, friends, and family, eventually impacting your relationships. Sleep deprived parents end up having major arguments over the littlest things, getting caught up in the blame game, wanting to be away from their spouses, and becoming very unhappy with one another within the first three years after their baby was born.

Sleep deprivation certainly affects your intimate and sexual connection with your spouse as well. Lack of sleep causes low energy, fatigue, and sleepiness, which affect libido and decreases interest in sex.

Health & Weight

Many people begin gaining a lot of weight when they are sleep deprived. A recent study found evidence suggesting that the nation's obesity epidemic is being driven, at least in part, by a consistent decrease in the average number of hours that we are sleeping, possibly by disturbing hormones that regulate appetite.

Several other reports, such as those from the Harvard Nurses' Health Study, link insufficient or irregular sleep to increased risk for colon cancer, breast cancer, heart disease, and diabetes. Additionally, aching muscles and nonspecific pain around the body are very common with sleep deprivation. **The first step to a healthy life is getting healthy sleep.**

Low Productivity & Effectiveness

When you are sleep deprived, your cognitive reasoning begins to suffer, and reaction times are severely compromised. Sleep deprivation impairs the quality and accuracy of your work, clear thinking and judgment, and the memory of important details. Sleep deprivation costs U.S. businesses nearly $150 billion annually in lost productivity. Your baby's sleep challenges are directly impacting your work performance.

Effect on Children

"Sleep is a vital asset for a child's health and overall development, learning, and safety."
- RICHARD L. GELULA
CEO, NATIONAL SLEEP FOUNDATION

Sleep deprivation affects all areas of your children's lives and every stage of their emotional, psychological, physical, intellectual, and cognitive development. The less healthy sleep that children get, the more likely they are to have growth deficiencies, to take longer to reach normal developmental milestones, to perform poorly in school, to have difficulty learning new things and retaining information, to become obese, to have a weaker immune system (and, therefore, to get sick more often), and to become depressed and to have a poor sense of self-worth.

Having healthy sleep habits and positive sleep associations from infancy are essential to your children's development, happiness, and success.

Growth and Development

The release of human growth hormone takes place during REM sleep. The release of this important hormone is the primary mechanism by which the human body induces growth. Because 80% of human growth hormone is released during sleep, the failure to achieve this sleep stage may negatively impact your baby's physical development and growth. Quality sleep is as important to building your baby's growing body as excellent nutrition.

Brain's Growth and Development

When a child is born, her newborn brain is only 30 percent of the size of an adult brain. During the first three years of a child's life, her brain grows rapidly, and it quickly increases to reach an almost-adult size. During this critical time, parents' decisions regarding baby's sleep habits have a huge and lasting impact on their child's brain development.

Just as the rest of the body responds to the release of human growth hormone during sleep, the brain is also dependent on the release of this hormone to grow. Because the brain can only grow during sleep, it is imperative that parents help their infant develop excellent sleep habits so that the growth and maturation process can occur.

Immune System & Health

Our immune system is designed to protect us from different ailments. Lack of sleep makes children's immune systems weaker and suppresses its functions, making them more prone to catching colds, viral infections, the flu and even worse illnesses. The first step to a healthy child is a good night's sleep.

Intelligence

Most parents have no idea that intelligence is linked to children's sleep habits. So, for those of you who needed an additional reason to teach your babies to sleep, this is a big one. Studies show that a great way to enhance a child's intelligence is encouraging healthy sleep patterns while he is a baby. Chronic sleep deprivation, sleep disruptions, and poor sleep habits that start at an early age have a lasting effect on cognitive performance, and they compromise learning abilities.

Memory

During the REM phase of sleep, the baby's brain assimilates and stores all the information that babies receive during their wakeful and alert hours. Babies are in an almost constant state of motor skill learning and coordination. They have a lot of new material to consolidate and, therefore, demand more sleep. Hence, sleep appears to play a key role in human development, and interferences to their REM sleep could undermine their learning.

Obesity

Sleep deprivation may make children more vulnerable to obesity, according to a new study. Sleeping less could serve as a trigger to the body to increase food intake and store fat. Additionally, insulin sensitivity and levels of two appetite-related hormones, leptin and ghrelin, can be affected by sleep deprivation, which could impact weight. Leptin is associated with appetite control, and ghrelin has been identified as an appetite stimulant. During sleep deprivation, leptin levels fall and ghrelin levels rise.

Obesity has doubled among children aged 2 to 5 in the past three decades; it has tripled among youths between the ages of 6 and 11; and it has also doubled in young people between the ages of 12 and 19. Insufficient nighttime sleep among children under 5 years of age appears to be a lasting risk factor for subsequent obesity.

Happiness, Depression & Self-Esteem

As I mentioned before, getting consistent, restful sleep is strongly correlated to being happy and feeling healthy—both mentally and emotionally. Sleep has a significant effect on a person's well-being. Continuous sleep deprivation in children can lead to clinical depression and low self-esteem.

Sleep results from changes in the balance of major neurotransmitters in the brain, such as serotonin, norepinephrine, dopamine, melatonin, and others. Many of these neurotransmitter systems are also responsible for multiple brain functions, including those related to mood and other cognitive and emotional behaviors. It is not surprising that significant interactions occur between sleep, depression, and happiness.

Sleep and Attention Deficit Disorder (ADD)

Research has shown that some kids are mislabeled with ADD when the real problem is sleep deprivation. Chronic poor sleep results in daytime tiredness, difficulty focusing attention, low threshold to expressing negative emotion, irritability, and easy frustration. These are the same symptoms that children diagnosed with Attention Deficit Hyperactivity Disorder show. When children show these symptoms, often no one thinks about the child's sleeping habits being the source of the problem.

Medical experts say that sleep deprivation and sleep disorders can cause ADHD and that by fixing a child's sleep problems, ADHD symptoms can be eliminated.

Chapter Five

SLEEP IS A LEARNED BEHAVIOR

"The beginning of a habit is like an invisible thread, but every time we repeat the act, we strengthen the strand, add to it another filament, until it becomes a great cable and binds us irrevocably, thought and act."

— ORISON SWETT MARDEN

I realize that a term like "sleep training" can make it seem like sleep is something that babies have to "learn." Sleep training is about helping your baby establish the good sleep habits that come naturally if we set up the right conditions for it. Babies have a real need to sleep, and they are capable of communicating this need to us. This process is innate, natural, and really not so complicated.

Parents, not babies, create bad habits by unconsciously fighting against what comes naturally to babies. This all occurs quite unintentionally, of course, but the problem can easily be remedied. Parents and children are equal partners in the sleep training process—both give and take cues from each other.

The habits children learn in sleeping start from day one. From birth and onwards, people learn habits of ways to fall asleep and stay asleep at night. These habits can be changed, and this is often the key to promoting healthy sleep in a child and avoiding certain sleep disorders.

> *The sleep patterns established when we are children*
> *will most likely last our lifetime.*

As you explore these resources, keep in mind that no two children are exactly alike. Every child is born with his or her own way of experiencing and approaching the world. This is typically described as someone's "temperament." Without question, **temperament shapes behavior and impacts sleep training.** Because of these important individual differences between children, it is impractical to offer one cookie-cutter strategy to sleep training that will work for everyone.

Also keep in mind that not all sleep disorders in children originate from learned habits and patterns and, therefore, not all can be addressed exclusively through sleep training and the development of healthy sleep habits. Some have to do with links to the child's central nervous system, and others have to do with other underlying medical conditions that your child might have. If you suspect that your child might be in that category, consult with your pediatrician or a medical sleep center.

HOW SLEEP WORKS

"Sleep is the golden chain that ties health and our bodies together."

- THOMAS DEKKER

Internal Biological Clock: Wake-Sleep Cycles

Children and adults have an internal biological clock that makes it easy to fall asleep at certain times and difficult to fall asleep at others. Although circadian rhythms are generated from within, they are also affected by signals from the environment. For the sleep cycle, the most important extraneous cue is sunlight.

There's a part of the brain that controls your body's internal clock, based on the information it gets from your eyes as to whether it is day or night. It regulates, accordingly, your bodily functions associated with sleep, including body temperature, urine production (bodies produce less urine while asleep, so that the need to urinate doesn't interrupt sleep), and changes in blood pressure.

Additionally, when the brain detects light, it signals the body to stop making melatonin (also known as the "sleep hormone"). When there is less light, the brain tells the body to increase the production of melatonin, which makes you feel sleepy. These changes that happen in the body over the course of a 24-hour period are called circadian rhythms. Among people with healthy circadian rhythms, there are morning people (aka "larks"), who prefer to sleep and wake early; night people (aka "owls"), who prefer to sleep and wake at late times; and everything in between.

Sleep Stages

Sleep is divided into two broad phases: rapid eye movement (REM) and non-rapid eye movement (Non-REM or NREM) sleep. Each type has a distinct set of associated physiological, neurological, and psychological features. Together, the stages of REM and Non-REM sleep form a complete sleep cycle that repeats until you wake up. Non-REM is further divided into three stages: N1, N2, and N3.

Non-REM Sleep

- **Stage N1 - Light Sleep**
  This is the first stage of true sleep. It lasts from 10 to 25 minutes. This sleep is very light. A gentle whisper, a soft touch, or a slight sound can wake you up. In this first stage, brain waves change from alpha waves of wakefulness to theta waves of sleep. Eye movement stops, heart rate slows, body temperature decreases, and muscles begin to relax slightly. Stage N1 makes up about **5% of total sleep** time in normal adult sleep.

- **Stage N2**

  This stage lasts about 30 to 60 minutes. It is not quite as easy to wake you up in this stage; and if you are awakened, you do not adjust immediately and often feel groggy and disoriented for several minutes. Eyes stop moving and muscles relax more. Stage N2 makes up about **50% of total sleep** time in normal adult sleep.

- **Stage N3 - Deep Sleep**

  This stage is also known as "delta sleep" or "slow-wave sleep." It tends to last for about 20 to 40 minutes in the first sleep cycle. It is the deepest stage of sleep. It is very hard to wake you up in this stage. Children tend to sleep more deeply than adults during stage N3, making it almost impossible to wake them up in their first slow-wave sleep of the night.

Brain waves are extremely slow, and blood flow is directed away from the brain and towards the muscles, restoring physical energy. The body repairs and regenerates tissues, builds bone and muscle, and appears to strengthen the immune system. There is an increase in delta waves. There may be some slight body movements toward the end of stage N3. It makes up about **20% of total sleep** time in normal adult sleep. Stage N3 sleep in children tends to be longer than in adults.

REM Sleep

REM Sleep - Dream Sleep

It takes place bout 70 to 90 minutes after onset. A newborn baby may go straight into stage REM sleep after falling asleep. The first sleep cycle of the night contains a REM sleep stage that lasts 1-10 minutes. REM sleep then tends to get longer during each of the following sleep cycles. The longest period of stage REM sleep may last for an hour near the end of the night.

Eyes tend to move rapidly, and heart rate, breathing, and blood pressure fluctuate. Brain waves move in a fast pattern. Intense dreaming occurs during REM sleep as a result of heightened brain activity. Our brain paralyzes many of our muscles during stage REM sleep. This protects us by preventing us from acting out on our dreams.

Interestingly enough, the neurological barrier that inhibits muscles in the legs and arms from contracting, is not fully developed in newborns. Without full inhibition, brain activity associated with REM sleep can result in dramatic twitches and movements of an infant's limbs. Some of these are strong enough to stir the child from sleep. Therefore, it also can be called "active sleep" in infants. Only during the second six months of life does the system develop sufficiently to inhibit dramatic body movements during REM sleep.

REM sleep is thought to assist in brain development, especially early in life. Not surprisingly, newborns and infants typically spend about twice as much time as adults in REM sleep. REM sleep makes up about **20-25% of total sleep** time in normal adult sleep and **50% of total sleep time in the normal sleep of**

infants. During the next few months of life, REM sleep tends to decrease. When a child reaches three months of age, the normal pattern of Non-REM sleep and REM sleep tends to take place. By age 10, a child has roughly the same percentage of stage REM sleep as an adult.

Sleep Cycles

Non-REM sleep and REM sleep continue to alternate throughout the night in a cyclical fashion. Sleep proceeds in cycles: N1 → N2 → N3 → N2 → REM. There is a greater amount of deep sleep (stage N3) earlier in the sleep cycle, while the proportion of REM sleep increases later in the sleep cycle and just before natural awakening.

The average length of the first Non-REM and REM sleep cycle is between 70 and 100 minutes; the average length of the second and later cycles is about 90 to 120 minutes in adults, and 50 minutes in children.

Chapter Seven

HEALTHY BABY SLEEP

"You are not healthy, unless your sleep is healthy."
- DR. WILLIAM DEMENT
FATHER OF SLEEP MEDICINE

Sleep habits are formed by a combination of developmental and behavioral factors. This chapter will help you understand what "healthy sleep" means to your baby. The first thing new parents should know about baby sleep is the difference between good and bad sleep or healthy and unhealthy sleep.

In order to understand "healthy sleep" in terms of what babies need, an explanation of the special sleep requirements that are unique to babies is essential. I define healthy baby sleep as the combination of three essential components:

- *One:* Number of Hours (Sleep Needs by Age)
- *Two:* Sleep Consolidation (Sleeping Through the Night)
- *Three:* Timing (Schedule Tailored to Your Baby)

Component 1: Right Number of Hours

The first component of healthy baby sleep is having the right number of hours for your baby. Studies show that children are being chronically sleep deprived, which is having devastating effects on them, and the parents are the only ones who can and should fix this problem.

Children have different sleep needs at different ages, and you need to have this in mind so that you have the right expectations. Every child is different and certain developmental milestones, personality, and family related circumstances might affect the amount of sleep they need; please take this information as a general guideline.

Age	Sleep Needs		
	Day (Hours)	Night (Hours)	Total (Hours)
0 – 2 Month	5 – 7	10 – 13	15 – 18
3 – 4 Months	4 – 5	10 – 12	14 – 16
5 – 6 Months	4 – 5	10 – 12	14 – 16
7 – 9 Months	2 – 4	11 – 13	13 – 15
10 – 12 Months	2 – 4	11 – 13	13 – 15
3 – 14 Months	2 – 3	11 – 13	13 – 15
15 – 18 Months	2 – 3	11 – 13	13 – 15
19 – 24 Months	2 – 3	10 – 13	12 – 15
2 – 3 Years	1 – 3	10 – 12	11 – 14
3 – 5 Years	0 – 2	10 – 12	11 – 13
5 – 11 Years	0	9 – 12	9 – 12
12 – 17 Years	0	8 – 11	8 – 11

Figure 1: Children's Sleep Needs by Age: Daytime and Nighttime Hours

Note: The hours from each column don't always add up since children might take shorter naps and sleep more hours at night and vice versa.

There is no such thing as "catching up on sleep." According to medical experts, once you lose out on sleep, it is gone. There is no "making it up" in terms of the effects on our mind and body. If children sleep in on weekends, it sets them up for sleep problems during the week. One of the best things that you can do for yourself and for your children is to have a consistent bedtime and waking time, based on your natural internal clock.

To download this table and have access to a more detailed version of it with the number of naps per age, the appropriate length and timing of each nap, expected night wakings, and essential information and tips on sleep transitions, go to our website www.SmoothBabySleepBook.com. Once there, click on the "Reference Tables & Guidelines" section and introduce the code SBSBOOK.

Signs of Sleep Deficiency in Children

Unlike adults who become lethargic, drowsy, and sleepy when sleep deprived, children more often become hyperactive. This hyperactivity masks their exhaustion, and it often makes it difficult for children to fall asleep at night, which in turn, creates even more sleep deprivation.

Every child is different; therefore, the way your child is signaling that he is sleep deprived and overtired might be completely different from the way another child would. However, these are common signs of sleep deprivation that your child might be showing:

- Constant daytime sleepiness and fatigue during the day
- Inattentiveness and lack of focus
- Impaired memory and cognitive ability (the ability to think and process information)
- Decreased academic performance
- Hyperactivity, over-activity, or excessive energy
- Crankiness and moodiness, especially at the end of the day
- Low threshold to express negative emotion
- Difficulty modulating impulses and emotions
- Difficult at bedtimes (taking more than 30-60 minutes to get your child to sleep at night, every night)
- Inability to stay sleep (frequent wakings during the night)
- Talking during sleep and/or sleep walking
- Nightmares, night terrors, and/or bedwetting
- Grinding and/or clenching one's teeth
- Difficulty getting up in the morning (It is difficult to get your child out of bed and active in the morning; and when he eventually wakes up, he is unhappy, fussing, and/or crying.)
- Early rising/waking up prematurely (4:45 a.m. to 5:30 a.m.)

While these are possible symptoms of sleep deprivation, they can also be symptoms of other chronic sleep disorders and other medical complications. Therefore, this is not meant to be a diagnostic list for sleep deprivation, but rather, it is a starting point.

Daytime Sleep - Naps

Daytime sleep is as important for our children as nighttime sleep is. I am still amazed when I hear some of the families that I work with mentioning that their pediatrician has told them that "naps are extra" or "optional." They are not. Naps might be optional for adults, but they are a MUST for children. They need those "breaks" during the day—not only to avoid getting overly tired, but also to recharge energy and continue growing and developing.

Therefore, naps should also be quality sleep not only quantity. To the extent possible, let your baby nap in a quiet, dark place, at the same time every day, and follow your naptime routine. (More on sleep environment in Chapter eight – Smooth Baby Sleep Approach / Step 1: Establish a Good Foundation.) Always protect the naps for as long as possible. Beware of letting your baby catnap throughout the day, as he might just be masking what otherwise would show as overtiredness. During the first weeks of life, catnaps are the norm, and you shouldn't worry about it. However, after the first 2-3 months of life, your child's naps should start lengthening, and the shortest nap of the day dropped. After the first 6 months of age, make sure your child's last nap is at least 3 hours before his bedtime.

The following table summarizes the recommended number of hours and number of naps by age.

Age	Day (Hours)	Number of Naps
0 – 2 Month	5 – 7	Several
3 – 4 Months	4 – 5	4 – 3
5 – 6 Months	4 – 5	3 – 2
7 – 9 Months	2 – 4	2
10 – 12 Months	2 – 4	2
13 – 14 Months	2 – 3	2
15 – 18 Months	2 – 3	2 – 1
19 – 24 Months	2 – 3	1
2 – 3 Years	1 – 3	1
3 – 5 Years	0 – 2	1 – 0
5 – 11 Years	0	0
12 – 17 Years	0	0

Figure 2: Children's Sleep Needs by Age – Daytime Sleep

You will find more information in detail on age by age considerations; the length of naps; when the right time for dropping the naps is; and sample schedules for every age on Part III – Customized Baby Sleep Approach / Step 2: Design your child's tailored schedule. Remember that you can download all these tables at www.SmoothBabySleepBook.com. Once there, click on the "Reference Tables & Guidelines" section and introduce the code SBSBOOK.

Component 2: Right Consolidation

The second component of healthy baby sleep is sleep consolidation. **Sleep consolidation**, in the context of baby sleep, is defined as the length of time your baby stays asleep during any given sleeping period. Just as your baby will require a different number of hours of sleep at different ages, he will also sleep for a different length of time depending on his age. A newborn's sleep is very irregular, where the need to sleep and the need to eat cycle during the day and night. After 3 or 4 months, baby sleep becomes consolidated into longer periods.

If you ask any new mother, she will probably tell you that the most common question she receives from others is, *"Is your baby sleeping through the night yet?"* So much importance is placed on this milestone that it can often become a source of frustration for first-time parents. But, **what does "sleeping through the night" really mean?**

Sleeping through the night refers to the longest stretch of sleep a child has during the night, which is equivalent to his maximum amount of night sleep consolidation. Sleeping through the night actually means different things at different ages.

Night sleep consolidation is influenced by factors like weight, family circumstances, health issues, and growth and development. Remember that newborns have very small stomachs that cannot hold large quantities of milk. As a result, babies under four months of age do not have the ability to sleep for prolonged stretches (sleep consolidation). Therefore, trying to force your baby into sleeping too many hours every night is not only physiologically difficult—it is also downright dangerous. By the time a baby reaches 18 months of age, "normal" sleep consolidation will have lengthened to roughly 11 to 12 hours of uninterrupted sleep at night, plus an additional 1- to 2-hour long nap each day

The following chart can be helpful for understanding the definition of "sleeping through the night" (night consolidations) at different ages. Keep in mind that this table provides only the guidelines for children who are healthy and reaching their developmental milestones. It is entirely conceivable that your two-month-old will begin sleeping 12 hours straight through the night, and your friend's six-month-old will still be only sleeping eight hours in one stretch. Both examples are well within the range of "normal" sleep consolidation for their ages. I encourage my clients to set a goal for their baby to be sleeping 12 hours at a time, through the night, between 4 to 6 months of age.

Age	Night Time Sleep	
	Night (Hours)	Sleeping Through the Night: Longest Stretch Without Waking (Number of Wakings)
0 – 2 Month	10 – 13	2.5 – 4 (many)
3 – 4 Months	10 – 12	4 – 8 (2 – 4)
5 – 6 Months	10 – 12	6 – 12 (0 –2)
7 – 9 Months	11 – 13	8 – 13 (0- 1)
10 – 12 Months	11 – 13	8 – 13 (0- 1)
13 – 14 Months	11 – 13	11 – 13
15 – 18 Months	11 – 13	11 – 13
19 – 24 Months	10 – 13	10 – 13
2 – 3 Years	10 – 12	10 – 12
3 – 5 Years	10 – 12	10 – 12
5 – 11 Years	9 – 12	9 – 12
12 – 17 Years	8 – 11	8 – 11

Figure 3: Children's Sleep Needs by Age: "Sleeping Through the Night" Guidelines

You can find a summary table, "Comprehensive Children's Sleep Needs by Age" combining all the information shown in the previous tables, in the Appendix of this book. To download it as a poster for easier reference in the future, you can go to visit www.SmoothBabySleepBook.com. Once there, click on the "Reference Tables & Guidelines" section and introduce the code SBSBOOK.

Component 3: Right Time for Your Baby

The third component of healthy baby sleep is trickier to establish because there is no "general" answer—it is to understand your baby's sleep patterns and his internal biological clock (see Chapter six – How Sleep Works, for further information) so that you can determine what times of the day are best suited for his naps and bedtime. This sleep schedule will be specific to your baby. Don't go against nature, but work with it to help your child become a great sleeper.

Large changes in sleep duration, naptime, and periods of alertness occur in a matter of weeks for children during their first months of life. Being aware that these shifts will occur is the best way to adjust expectations and prepare for an adaptive and tailored schedule. One of the first steps I ask new parents to complete is observing the natural sleep and wake habits of their child, by tracking them and taking detailed notes about when naps and nighttime sleep occur and about the general demeanor of their child after each rest period.

- Is your baby happier right after he wakes up?

- Does she become fussy towards lunchtime?

- Does she get whiny or clingy before dinnertime?

- Does she take too short or too long naps?

It is important to keep track of any of your observations about the behavior and mood of your child throughout the day. Your goal is to "learn" your child, how her unique internal body clock works, and how she is signaling you when it's time for her to eat, sleep, or play.

Based on your findings, you will be able to understand what times of the day are more favorable for a nap or set bedtime, and you'll be able to create a customized, adaptive schedule. Remember, there are basic principles that work with every child, but your child is special and one-of-a-kind. **Excellent parents customize good advice to meet the unique needs of their unique child**. We will go over the processes of creating a schedule in great detail in Chapter eight: Smooth Baby Sleep Approach/ Step 2: Design Your Child's Tailored Schedule.

As I mentioned before, you can find a cheat sheet with all the information about children's sleep needs in the Appendix of this book. To download it as a poster for easier reference in the future, you can go to www.SmoothBabySleepBook.com. Once there, click on the "Reference Tables & Guidelines" section and introduce the code SBSBOOK.

෨ Jazmine and Bella: 15-month-old premature twins

Jazmine and Bella were born prematurely, at 29 weeks gestation. They spent the first months of their lives in the Neonatal Intensive Care Unit, went through several surgeries, and were finally discharged with apnea monitors and high-risk health concerns. They went through several emergency runs to the hospital. They had difficulty breathing, and mom had to do cardio-pulmonary resuscitation (CPR) on them—but they made it. By the time they were 9 months, these precious children were still tiny, still trying to catch up in weight, but were finally healthy. However, due to the understandable stress and health concerns, they weren't able to develop healthy sleep habits and the ability to self-soothe and fall asleep on their own.

By the time they were 15 months old, the situation was almost unbearable for their caring and dedicated parents, Maria and Daniel. Jazmine and Bella had never slept in their cribs, and they had never slept through the night. One of them slept in a co-sleeper, and the other slept in the parent's bed. They couldn't fall asleep on their own, and they woke up multiple times during the night, every night. They both napped at different times, always in the parent's bed, with mom lying down with them. As Maria mentioned during our first conversations, *"We are completely drained out and exhausted."* They couldn't function properly during the day.

We went through the process that I am walking you through in this book, and made sure I understood what their main challenges goals were. They wanted Jazmine and Bella to sleep on their cribs, to have a consistent day schedule, and to be happier and less cranky during the day.

I came up with a customized schedule and a plan for them. The first night was hard, as Maria and Daniel learned the new approach and the whole family adjusted to the changes. However, the progress was quicker than any of us had anticipated. The second night, Bella slept through the night without waking up; and the third night, Jazmine joined her. The family was able to put an end to 15 months of struggles and sleep deprivation. Jazmine and Bella were sleeping 12 hours through the night and napping another 2 hours daily—and they were happier during the day.

PART III:

YOUR CHILD'S CUSTOMIZED SMOOTH SLEEP PLAN

Chapter Eight

SMOOTH BABY SLEEP APPROACH

""Do this every night with an 'I Love you': Always kiss your children goodnight—even if they're already asleep."
— H. BROWN, JR.

When you hear the term "sleep training," what images come to mind? Traumatized days-old infants left to "cry it out?" If that's the case, you are not alone. Many parents associate "sleep training" with mandating that babies are required to "cry it out" so that they will "sleep through the night." The American Academy of Pediatrics argues that if you let your baby fuss and even cry for as much as fifteen to twenty minutes, she'll learn to get herself to sleep without relying on you. However, that is not the only sleep training method out there; in fact, that is the only method out there that I would *never* recommend you to follow.

I strongly believe that **no two children are exactly alike**, and that is the main pillar of Smooth Baby Sleep Approach. Every child is different, and every family is different. Parents all have different parenting approaches, and I have to honor those. I also know that happy parents equal happy children. Because of these important individual differences between children, **it's impossible**

54

**to offer one sleep training strategy and one schedule that will
work for every child**.

In this chapter, you will design and customized your child's
Smooth Baby Sleep Plan, which combines the best aspects of
traditional sleep training and tailored scheduling with sensitivity to
ensuring that your child's *real needs* are always met. My method will
never push you into doing something that doesn't resonate with
your parenting style, your lifestyle, your child's personality, and his
own individual circumstances.

The following chapters in the book are structured in the
same way that the Smooth Baby Sleep Approach is. The approach
follows the promised 6 simple steps to gently help your child sleep.

DESIGN

Step 1 -   Establish   a   Good   Foundation:
             Golden Pillars of Smooth Baby Sleep

Step 2 -   Design a Tailored Schedule

Step 3 -   Choose the Best Sleep Coaching
             Method for Your Child

Step 4 -   Apply Age-by-Age Considerations

Step 5 -   Put It All Together: Build Your
             Child's Customized Plan

IMPLEMENTATION

Step 6 -   Make It Happen & Follow Through

By the end of this section, you will have your child's fully
customized Smooth Sleep Plan and will know how to best put it
into practice.

DESIGN

Step One

ESTABLISH A GOOD FOUNDATION: GOLDEN PILLARS OF SMOOTH BABY SLEEP

"We must learn to accept the fact that during their developmental years children cannot be expected to exhibit adult behavior."

- ROBERT MENDELSOHN, M.D.

As you have probably guessed by now, I am a firm believer in the importance of respecting the differences in each child, while ensuring that specific "best practices" of sleep training take place. In my experience working with a variety of families, the following 5 "Golden Pillars of Smooth Baby Sleep" are imperative and the first step towards helping your child develop healthy sleep habits and learn to self-soothe:

1. *Right Expectations and Goals*
2. *Appropriate Attitude and Mindset*
3. *Calming, Bonding, and Safe Sleep Rituals*
4. *Safe and Soothing Sleep Haven*
5. *Everyone on Board*

It is essential that you have them in mind as you move forward in helping your child sleep better.

1. Right Expectations and Goals

Have you taken a moment to consider your expectations for sleep training your child? During my private consultations with parents, I generally advise moms and dads to keep in mind what their goals are for the sleep training process. I invite you to consider the main goals that I always have in mind before I design a family's sleep strategy. These are the things that you should make sure happen at the end of your child's sleep training process:

✓ *Ensuring Your Child Gets Healthy Baby Sleep*
✓ *Producing an Independent Sleeper*
✓ *Preserving the Parent-Child Bond*

Healthy Baby Sleep

If you recall from chapter seven, healthy baby sleep is defined as the right number of hours, with the right sleep consolidation, happening at the right time for your baby. Combining these three components produces the type of quality rest that is truly restorative to your baby. Please go back and read that section of chapter seven and check how many hours of sleep your child needs per day, both day and night, and what the right consolidation is for him.

You can find a summary table with that information in the Appendix section of this book and on this book's website www.SmoothBabySleepBook.com. Once there, click on the "Reference Tables & Guidelines" section and introduce the code SBSBOOK, and download a copy of that cheat sheet for you to have as a constant reference as your child grows up.

Independent Sleeper

The main goal of sleep training is to help our children become independent sleepers. An independent sleeper is one who falls asleep on his own and puts himself back to sleep when he wakes up. This means that while you can still cuddle, rock, nurse, or pat your child as part of his bedtime (and naptime) routine, he doesn't require those actions to fall asleep.

I would also add that a "real" independent sleeper is one "for life." This means that a real independent sleeper will not need to be "retrained" to sleep when major things happen: he is moved to a toddler bed, starts preschool, is potty training, etc. In order to create a "real independent sleeper," you need to help them establish **right, healthy, reassuring, and positive sleep associations**.

You might know by now that babies are very noisy sleepers, so when they start fussing in the middle of the night, wait a ½ minute or so to go check on them. Learn to differentiate between "sleepy sounds" and cries for help. If you go check on her when she's doing the sleepy sounds, you risk waking her up. Do not respond to every tiny noise your baby makes when she's sleeping.

Strong & Intact Parent-Child Bond

Bonds are created when parents successfully meet their children's needs—whether it is changing a wet diaper, filling up a hungry tummy, or comforting a fear. If a child is forced to cry all night without being comforted by a parent until he falls asleep, his needs are not being met. Naturally, this situation leads to a compromised parent-child bond.

Of course, you want your baby to become an independent sleeper, but you do not want the price you pay for that to be your relationship with your child. Your child trusts you completely and sees you as his constant protector. The sleep training process should not get in the way of that bond and trust. When I am working with my sleep-coaching clients, I always keep this relationship forefront in my mind and in the minds of the parents.

While I want your child to become an independent sleeper and self-soothe, I don't want him to feel abandoned when it's time to sleep. I still want him to be able to call for you (by crying, or actually calling you), when he really needs you (he's in pain, he's hungry, he's got a soiled diaper, etc.), and know that you will be there to help him. I want your child to be certain that he can trust you to be there for him when he really needs you, especially as he learns that when it's time to sleep, it's time to sleep. Through working with many families, I have learned that the "cry-it-out" method does not enhance trust, reassurance, and bonding, and this is the main reason I do not advocate its use.

Mom and Dad, if you take time to set positive, realistic goals and to review how long it usually takes to sleep train (see section above and chapter eight) before implementing the Smooth Baby Sleep method, you will have a yardstick by which to measure future success. If your expectations revolve around ensuring your baby gets healthy baby sleep, producing an independent sleeper, creating positive sleep associations, and most importantly, preserving the parent-child bond, you can be assured that your baby's sleep training process will be positive and beneficial to your entire family.

2. Appropriate Attitude & Mindset

Be Calm, Patient & Nurturing

Every time I work with a new mom on a private consultation, the first thing I do before implementing anything or talking about plans is to make sure that mom and dad are in the right place emotionally. You can't give what you don't have; to be there for your child, you have to be there for you.

Believe me when I say, I know how frustrated and exhausted you feel right now. But, remember that you are your baby's whole world, and surrounding him with love, nurture, and guidance starts by you having the right attitude when you are with your child. Your attitude and the energy that you project affect the outcome of your baby's sleep coaching process.

Some parents I've worked with admitted to having put their babies in their cribs or bassinets a little bit too harshly, out of anger and desperation for sleep. If you are angry, anxious, frustrated, defeated, or agitated, your baby will sense that, and that will make it harder for him to fall asleep. Please, **be patient and always enter your baby's room in a calm state**. If you feel overwhelmed; your patience is evaporating; you are exhausted; you can't take it anymore; and you think you might be reaching your breaking point, please follow these steps:

1. Place your baby calmly and softly on a safe place (crib, bassinet, stroller, bouncy seat, etc.).
2. Back off—step away to another room, go to the bathroom and wash your face, or open the window and breathe some fresh air.

3. Ask for help from your spouse, a family member, a friend, or even a neighbor.
4. Calm yourself down before picking up your baby again.

Changing a habit takes time. Sleeping is an innate ability to babies; parents, without any bad intentions, create poor or unhealthy sleep habits that need to be addressed later on. **Remind yourself that you helped your child get into this situation (habit), and now you have to help him get out of it.**

Do NOT ever shake or hit your baby! (For more information on this read over Chapter four/ Effect On Parents)

To help mothers cope with the stress of becoming a new parent, I launched a relaxation and empowerment audio guide for new mothers, titled "I Am the Mom I've Always Wanted to Be." In this audio, I guide you through positive daily affirmations that will help you be the best parent you can be, the great mother your child deserves. It also includes relaxation techniques, bonding exercises, and much more. To get your copy, visit the website www.SmoothParenting.com

Be Open-Minded and Willing

As you continue reading and diving into the Smooth Baby Sleep Approach, I ask you to make the commitment to be open-minded, because if your mind is closed, you won't be able to learn. Some of my ideas, approaches, comments, or philosophies might make you feel uneasy or uncomfortable, and that is fine. If you continue doing what's comfortable or easy or what you've been doing until now, you will continue getting the same results. In fact, Albert Einstein defined insanity as "doing the same thing over and over again and expecting different results." So, if you want different results with regards to your child's sleep, if you want your child to become an independent sleeper with positive sleep associations and healthy sleep habits, you have to change what you've been doing until now.

Many parents self-sabotage by saying, "*I already know that.*' You might have heard about or read about some of these concepts and ideas, but the key is how those concepts are combined, adapted to your family, and consistently implemented in your child's life. We also self-sabotage by falling prey to the "*Yes, but...*" syndrome. "*Yes, but that won't work for my kids.*" "*Yes, but they have help and I don't.*" "*Yes, but I don't have time for that.*" All of which is basically a mechanism to give excuses to ourselves to not try new things or implement change.

Be Consistent

Being inconsistent in our approach and responses is one of the worst things that we can do as parents, because it is impossible for our children to learn what to do when we are giving them mixed signals. This inconsistency of responses is called **"intermittent reinforcement"** in behavioral psychology.

Imagine for a moment that you go to a children's store with your child to buy her new pajamas. On your way to the clothing section, you pass by the toy section, and your child asks you to buy her a toy. You say "no" and keep moving. Within a couple of minutes, your child has forgotten all about the toy and is happy again. You buy your child's pajamas, and pass by the toy section again. Your child starts crying because she wants that toy. You say "no" again, and keep walking. When you are almost by the check-out counter, you remember that you also had to buy diaper rash cream, so you go back in and walk by the toy section a third time. Your child starts crying more and more. Still, you say "no" again, and continue walking to get the diaper rash cream. On your way back, you run into a friend, and you both continue walking together to the checkout counter. When you pass by the toy section again, your child looses it and starts crying, screaming, and kicking. You want to continue talking to your friend, and you are feeling a little embarrassed from the scene that your child is causing. You cave in, give her the toy, and continue on your way to the check-out counter.

A couple of weeks later, you find yourself having to go the same children's store to buy diapers. The first time you pass by the toy section, your child asks for a toy, and you say "no." Your child starts crying. This time it doesn't stop after a couple of minutes; her fit goes on and on and on. She gets more and more agitated with every step you take. Why do you think this is happening? Because that's what you've taught her the last time you were there with her. You've taught her that if she cries long enough and hard enough, she will get what she wants.

Now, what's the best course of action in this situation? Obviously, sticking to your position—if you said "no," you mean "no." She won't be very happy about it, and the next couple of times you will go to the store with her, she will most likely have another fit. This situation could've been avoided if the first time you went to the store with her you had kept your word, regardless of how upset she got.

Everything in parenting comes down to being consistent. If you are not consistent, things will be not only harder on you but also harder on your child, because she will not understand why you're doing what you're doing and what's expected of her. Your response has to always be the same. If you don't want to co-sleep with your child, then your bed cannot be an option for her—not even at 4 a.m. when you're already exhausted and just want to get some sleep. If you don't want to have to nurse your child to sleep, then you can't use nursing to get him back to sleep in a couple of minutes in the middle of the night.

Whatever approach you use to sleep train your child, make sure you are consistent and that you give it at least 7-10 consecutive days before deciding whether it's working. Do not try a different method every other night. **The more mixed signals, the more different methods, the more inconsistent you are with your child; the longer and harder the process is going to be, and the more tears you are going to get**.

Make Sleep a Priority

Even though, we know how important baby sleep is, we sometimes let life, commitments, self-imposed compromises, friends, family, work, and even pets get in the way of our baby getting healthy sleep. More often than not, I hear the moms I work with tell me, *"My mother-in-law came to see the baby, so I had to wake her up to see Grandma."* Or, *"My friends always have a play date when my son's naptime is, so he always skips that nap."* Or, *"My husband doesn't get home from work until 8 p.m. and he really wants to see his daughter and spend some time with her before putting her to sleep, so she never goes to bed before 9 p.m."* All those are examples of how we let other things become more important than our child's sleep.

Most of us wouldn't use the same excuses when it comes to feeding our baby—even though the average person could go 4-6 weeks without food, and only 10-12 days without sleep. I don't think I've ever heard a mom say, *"My mother in law came to see the baby, so I had to stop feeding her to see grandma."* Or, *"My friends always have a play date when my son's lunch is, so he always skips that meal."* Or,

"My husband doesn't get home from work until 8 p.m., and he really wants to have dinner with his daughter; so she has dinner at 9 p.m."

Let Your Baby Sleep

It sounds simple, but it usually isn't. Do not feel obligated to have your baby wake up because you have visitors. Do not disturb your baby's sleep because you have company. Do not try to keep your baby awake so that you can play with her a little longer. And, do not try to build your child's sleeping schedule around your life. Instead, build it around her natural internal clock.

The quality and quantity of your baby's sleep directly impacts all areas of her life. **Don't let anything or anyone (including you or your spouse) get in the way of your baby getting healthy sleep.**

Don't Expect Miracles

Devote time and effort to make sure that your children get enough and proper sleep; it will be a fantastic health gift for life. No sleep method or sleep consultant can guarantee overnight results; and if they do, be suspicious. In other words, no method will have your baby happily sleeping on his own, straight through the night the first night of sleep training. It takes an average of two weeks to change a habit, and it takes time for our children to adjust to the changes.

3. Calming, Bonding, and Safe Sleep Rituals

"Sleep patterns and sleep routines matter because they have both long-term and short-term implications for health and cognitive development. [...] If it sets a pattern in the way you treat sleep or bedtime, these patterns may last your whole life unknowingly."

- LAUREN HALE,
MD, PREVENTIVE MEDICINE

Sometimes, it is easy to forget your tiny baby is actually a little person with thoughts, feelings, and expectations of her own. If you are consistent in your parenting, children very quickly begin to anticipate the natural flow of the day based on what you have done in the past. **Our children should not associate sleep with feelings of abandonment, fear, desperation, anxiety, punishment, excitement, or stimulation. Instead, sleep should be associated with feelings of tranquility, relaxation, love, trust, restfulness, empowerment, and peace**.

Creating positive sleep associations is a relatively simple process if you are mindful that your baby will form a connection, or association, with the activities that occur directly before you place her to sleep and after she wakes up. You can avoid creating negative sleep associations from the first day if you keep your baby's sleep goals in mind. Note that I said "sleep routines," not only bedtime routines. Your baby's naptime routine is just as important for your baby as the bedtime routine is.

A large part of creating positive sleep associations is crafting sleep time routines that will reinforce good sleep habits.

Developing a soothing and calming routine that helps your baby transition from awake to sleep is an essential part of your sleep training process. Setting sleep routines can improve sleep quality and quantity for infants and toddlers, and it's a fantastic way to bond and cuddle with your child. A child's sleep routines could affect her sleep pattern throughout a lifetime. Your goal is to teach your child the process to fall asleep and to help her feel safe, secure, and comforted. **If the feeling around bedtime is a good feeling, your child will fall asleep easier.**

Additionally, one of the main concerns parents have with regards to their baby's sleep (besides helping him to sleep) is safety, specifically Sudden Infant Death Syndrome (SIDS). There are many things parents can do to help reduce the risk of SIDS, and I will cover them all in this section.

Sudden Infant Death Syndrome (SIDS)

SIDS is the unexpected, unpredictable, unexplained, sudden death of a seemingly healthy child. Most SIDS deaths occur in children between 2 and 4 months of age, rarely occurring before 1 month of age or after 6 months. Infants who die from SIDS show no signs of suffering.

SIDS is the leading cause of death among infants 1 to 12 months old. SIDS causes roughly 2,500 deaths per year in the US.

In most cases, the parent or caregiver puts the baby down to sleep and later discovers that he has died. You can help reduce your infant's risk by following some of the recommendations in this section of the book.

The following are guidelines to establish healthy and safe sleep routines that you should have in mind when helping your child establish positive sleep associations.

Back to Sleep

Not too long ago, pediatricians and other health care providers used to think that babies should sleep on their stomachs. However, research now shows that healthy babies are less likely to die of Sudden Infant Death Syndrome (SIDS) when they sleep on their backs. Therefore, placing your baby on his or her back to sleep is the number one way to reduce the risk of SIDS.

Every sleep time counts, so do not make exceptions to this rule for short naps. Additionally, make sure that all caregivers place your baby to sleep in the same position. Let everyone putting your baby to sleep (spouse, grandparents, babysitters, nanny, daycare team, friends, etc.) know about the best positioning, and guarantee that they all place your baby to sleep in the same way.

Studies show that babies who are used to sleeping on their backs, but who are occasionally then placed on their stomachs or sides to sleep, are at significantly higher risk of SIDS. This risk is greater (sometimes, seven to eight times greater) than that of infants who are always placed on their stomachs or sides to sleep.

Once a baby has the ability to roll over, the neck muscles are stronger and the risk of SIDS decreases. When infants roll over on their own, there is no evidence showing that they need to be repositioned back to their backs.

Build Tummy Time in Your Child's Schedule

After the "back to sleep" campaign was launched worldwide to prevent SIDS, our babies started spending more time on their backs. They are on their backs while they're sitting in their car seats, strollers, swings, and bouncy seats, and now, they are also lying on their backs when they are sleeping. Because they are spending so much time on their backs, it is essential for parents to offer them more tummy time during their awake hours every day. A minimum of 30 minutes per day is essential.

Tummy time helps prevent flat head syndrome (positional plagiocephaly) and neck twisting or arching (torticollis), which have become more common lately. Tummy time also helps your child build her core muscles, neck muscles, arm muscles, and shoulder muscles, which are essential for major developmental milestones, such as crawling, pushing up, rolling over, sitting up, self-feeding, and pulling to a stand.

Swaddling

Swaddle your baby from the time when he comes home from the hospital. The main purpose of swaddling your baby while she's a newborn is to make her feel secure, warm, and safe. After nine months inside your womb, your baby will feel disoriented in the outside world. Swaddling will help her remember her previous environment and rest.

Swaddle your baby in a breathable blanket that is large enough to cover your baby and appropriate for the current weather conditions. As a rule of thumb, remember that babies should wear one more layer than adults, so do not overdress your baby, as overheating is a major risk factor for SIDS.

After two to three months, many babies will start kicking and fighting the swaddle, while others are comfortable being "wrapped" until about 4 months. Whenever you see your baby fighting the swaddling while he's sleeping or before falling asleep, it's your cue to stop swaddling.

Swaddling a baby becomes a safety hazard once your baby is able to roll over, which usually occurs between 2 and 5 months. Stop swaddling once your baby learns how to roll over. You don't want your baby to roll from his back to his tummy in the crib and end up swaddled face down. Therefore, once you notice that your baby can roll from his back to his tummy, stop swaddling.

Pacifier During Sleep Time

It is totally natural for babies to suck on something, whether it is the thumb, a finger, or a pacifier. Sucking is a way that babies and toddlers soothe themselves. The American Academy of Pediatrics and I recommend the use of pacifiers for sleep during the first 6 to 12 months of life, as it has been proven to decrease the risk of SIDS. If you choose to follow my advice to offer your baby a pacifier, keep these tips in mind:

- If you are planning on breastfeeding your baby, wait until it is well established to introduce the pacifier.
- Offer a pacifier during sleep time and avoid it for the rest of the day.
- Pacifiers should not be coated in anything.
- Once your baby has settled on a favorite pacifier, keep several identical backups on hand.
- "Grow" the pacifier with your child. In other words, increase the size of your child's pacifier as he grows up.

- Replace pacifiers often and watch for signs of deterioration. Look for discoloration, holes, tears, and weak or sticky spots that could cause the nipple to tear off when sucked, putting your baby at risk of choking. Pacifiers are relatively inexpensive; therefore, I recommend replacing them at the smallest sign of deterioration.
- Choose the one-piece, dishwasher-safe variety. Pacifiers made of two pieces pose a choking hazard if they break.
- Keep the pacifier clean. Before you offer it to your baby, wash it with soap and water and let it to dry completely. Avoid "cleaning" the pacifier in your own mouth (or anybody else's mouth), as you might spread germs to your baby.
- Do not use pacifier clips, strings, ribbons, cords, etc. when placing your baby to sleep, as they can end up wrapped around your baby's neck, finger, hand, or arm and cut blood flow, posing a suffocation and strangulation hazard. If you decide to use them when your baby is awake, make sure the strap isn't long enough to get caught around your baby's neck, and always keep an eye on your baby while using them.
- If the pacifier falls out of your baby's mouth, try not to put it back in. If your child is old enough to hold the pacifier and bring it to his mouth, teach him how to do it instead of doing it for him. If your child is mobile enough to be able to move around the crib to find the pacifier, teach him how to do that, instead of searching for the pacifier yourself and giving it to your child.
- You might begin to wean your child from a pacifier at age 6 months to 12 months. Most children stop sucking on thumbs, pacifiers, or other objects on their own between 2 and 4 years of age. Therefore, you can also allow your child to self-wean from the pacifier, as long as he's only

using it to sleep, and they do so by the time they are 3 or 4, when permanent changes in the jaws start taking place.

No External Sleep "Helpers"

I do not recommend you to use music, sound machines, or white noise machines to help get your child to sleep. I believe in teaching children to become **independent sleepers**. I want them to be able to fall asleep without help and without the help of any external "aide" that might not always be available to them.

I would rather see a child who doesn't need anything external to fall asleep, than to see a child who needs to hear music or to have a white noise machine on in order to fall asleep. However, if you need or want to have it anyway, make sure:

- It doesn't turn off. You don't want to have to get out of bed in the middle of the night just to turn on a white noise machine or to turn the music back on because your baby woke up and can't fall back to sleep without it.
- It is portable so that you can bring it with you when visiting family or friends or when traveling with your baby.

In some specific circumstances, I might recommend their use, but certainly not for every child. I understand that in some cases, white noise machines can help babies sleep better, since they cancel out household or city noises that might interfere with their sleep. In those cases, I would recommend you to use them if your baby has shown signs of not being able to fall asleep due to those disturbances or if they are disrupting his sleep.

Drowsy, but Awake

When your baby is a newborn, she will more than likely fall asleep in your arms before you have the opportunity to put her down to sleep, "drowsy." If this occurs, don't worry, and don't try to wake her back up. Instead, just try the next time to put her down to sleep while she is "drowsy, but awake," as your goal is to help her learn how to self-soothe. In any case, you should never let your baby cry herself to sleep, especially while she's under 4 months of age.

Let your child lay awake in their cribs during the day, standing right next to them of course, for a couple of minutes at a time so that she learns that there's nothing wrong with being awake in the crib.

Soothing and Long-lasting Sleep Routines

Following the same steps before putting him to sleep for naps and bedtime will cue her that it's time to sleep. The bedtime routine should be a time for you to interact with your child in a way that is calming and loving.

Spend some special time with your child, let them know you love her and that you are going to be there for her. Most people think that when you're teaching your baby to sleep, you can't cuddle anymore; you can't rock her; you can't sing to her and hold her—not true! After two years, I still hold and rock my daughters at bedtime every night, while we sing "Twinkle, Twinkle, Little Star," and they are wonderful, independent sleepers. You can still have those bonding moments and rituals with your child—just make sure you stop before she falls asleep.

Keep it short. Your child's naptime routine should last 5-15 minutes, and her bedtime routine should last 15-30 minutes, excluding her bath. Your child's sleep routine need not take place in its entirety in your child's bedroom, but it should culminate there such that the last 15 minutes are in the bedroom where the child will sleep.

There is a major connection between time in front of the screen and sleep disorders. **Avoid television watching, video game playing, and other exciting activities the hour before bedtime**. Do not allow children to have a TV in their bedroom, and do not allow them to watch TV prior to bedtime. Children who watch a lot of television, especially at bedtime, and those with a television in their bedroom are more likely to resist going to bed, have trouble sleeping, wake up more often, and have a poor quality sleep overall. Watching television tends to stimulate children, whereas for adults it can be relaxing. Do not allow children to watch violent television programs. They can contribute to restless sleep and nightmares (among other things). Similarly, video games can impact a child's quality and amount of sleep. Do not allow children to play video games anywhere near bedtime and always check the appropriateness of the rating.

Don't change your child's routine every day, but let it evolve as your baby grows. For example, your bedtime routine with your newborn might involve giving him a bath, massaging him, putting him in his pajamas, giving him a bottle (or nursing him), rocking him a little, and putting him in the crib. By the time your child is 9 months, it might evolve to giving him a bath, massaging him, putting him in his pajamas, giving him a bottle (or nursing him) while you sing to him, giving him his lovey and putting him in the crib. By the time your child is 2 years old, it might evolve to giving him a bath, putting him in his pajamas, brushing his teeth, reading him a book, giving him his lovey, and putting him in the crib.

Finally, **don't start anything that you are not willing to continue down the road**. If you know you don't want to co-sleep, don't bring your baby to your bed. If you won't want to have to rock your baby to sleep when she is two years old, don't do it when she is 2 months old. If you don't want to have to nurse your baby to sleep in the middle of the night, do not nurse him to sleep at bedtime. Be aware of the associations that you create with sleep from day one, and make sure you only establish healthy and sustainable ones.

4. Safe and Soothing Sleep Haven

Your baby's sleep environment, attire, and rituals must be soothing and calming. The associations that your child has with his sleep environment should be positive, nurturing, loving, calming, and comforting.

Create a Soothing & Sleep-conducive Room

You want your child's room to be **dark**. On a scale from one to ten, ten being pitch black, you want your child's nursery to be around a seven or eight. If you decide to leave on a night-light, make sure it's not too bright, but gives enough light for your child to see his surroundings.

Your child's nursery should be **quiet** and away from the main activity area of your home. You don't need to be whispering while your baby naps or sleeps, but she shouldn't be exposed to loud noises while sleeping.

Keep your baby's nursery between 68 to 72 degrees F. Higher temperatures have been proven to increase the risk of SIDS, so make sure your baby is properly dressed and keep that temperature. The best way to see if your baby's temperature is adequate, touch his chest, underneath his clothes. If his chest is warm and fine, that means he is fine, even if his hands or nose might be cold.

Dress your baby in flame-resistant and snug-fitting sleep clothes. You can cover your baby with a sleep sack as mentioned above. When choosing a sleep bag, make sure the width of the neck isn't wide enough for your child to slip himself completely in.

Keep the nursery **aired.** Avoid exposing your baby to tobacco smoke, and do not smoke or let anyone smoke around your baby.

Set up a Good Baby Monitor

Have a good baby monitor installed in your baby's nursery so that you don't have to go in the nursery to check on your baby every time he fusses. Even if you are within hearing distance, I would recommend you to have a good monitor.

I am a believer in guaranteeing parents' "peace of mind," so choose the monitor that will give you the most peace of mind. If you think you will need to "see" your baby, get a video monitor; if you think you will be too stressed about your baby not moving, get a monitor with a movement sensor. Whatever you think you will need, to feel that your baby is safe and that you would be able to recognize when he's in trouble, make sure the monitor takes care of it.

The baby monitor cords can present a strangulation hazard to children if placed too close to a crib. Because of this serious strangulation risk, you should never place the monitors (and other corded gadgets) within three feet of your child's crib.

For lists of recommended baby monitors, and other product reviews, visit our website:

www.SmoothParenting.com.

Put Your Baby to Sleep On His Crib

In general, I would argue that the best place for a baby to sleep is in her own crib or bassinet (if your baby is less than six months old and is not yet able to push up to her hands and knees), in your room during the first months of life and in her own bedroom after the first three to six months of age. Infants who sleep in the same room, though not in the same bed, as their mothers have a lower risk of SIDS. However, it is your decision as a parent whether this is the right thing for you and your family.

I have nothing against co-sleeping or family bed sharing, as long as it is done in a safe way and it is the best solution for the family. It wasn't the best solution for my family, but that doesn't mean it's not the best solution for yours. Before I delve into the pros and cons of crib sleeping and co-sleeping, I would like to make sure you understand that I am using the terms co-sleeping and bed-sharing as interchangeable, even though I know co-sleeping can also be used when your baby is placed in a co-sleeper attached to your bed.

Many people think that children who co-sleep with their parents can't develop healthy sleep habits, but that's not true. In fact, I have worked with multiple co-sleeping families, who wanted to continue co-sleeping but who wanted their babies to become independent sleepers and have healthier sleep habits.

Many parents struggle with the issue of allowing their infant to sleep in their bed with them. **Proponents of co-sleeping** argue that the dangers of an infant sleeping in an adult bed are exaggerated and that many cultures around the world have engaged in this practice for centuries. Co-sleeping encourages breastfeeding by making nighttime breastfeeding more convenient and makes it easier for a nursing mother to get her sleep cycle in sync with her baby's. Having said that; I want to point that it tends to be more difficult to night-wean co-sleeping babies, since nursing is not only a feeding activity but also a soothing mechanism.

The close and warm contact can help the baby fall asleep quicker and sleep more soundly. However, sharing a bed with your child can sometimes prevent parents and children from getting a good night's sleep. Infants who co-sleep learn to associate sleep with being close to a parent in the parent's bed, which may become a problem at naptime or when the infant needs to go to sleep before the parent is ready or when the parent is not home.

Opponents of co-sleeping argue that there are inherent dangers that cannot be ignored. The U.S. Consumer Product Safety Commission (CPSC) warns parents not to place their infants to sleep in adult beds, stating that the practice puts babies at risk of suffocation and strangulation; and the American Academy of Pediatrics (AAP) agrees.

Adult beds as they are, are not safe for infants. A baby can easily become trapped and suffocate between the headboard slats, the space between the mattress and the bed frame, or the space between the mattress and the wall. A baby could also suffocate if a sleeping parent accidentally rolls over and covers the baby's nose and mouth or if he ends up under the sheets, pillows, or comforters that adults have in their bed. Co-sleeping is a widespread practice in many non-Western cultures. However, differences in mattresses, bedding, and other cultural practices may account for the lower risk in these countries as compared with the United States.

The connection between co-sleeping and SIDS is unclear and research is ongoing. Some co-sleeping researchers have suggested that it can reduce the risk of SIDS because co-sleeping parents and babies tend to wake up more often throughout the night. However, the AAP reports that some studies suggest that, under certain conditions, co-sleeping may increase the risk of SIDS.

Co-sleeping fosters a positive family image that the unit can relate to and spending this special time together strengthens invisible bonds. Against general beliefs, co-sleeping does not correlate with low self-esteem, low independence, poor social skills, or unhealthy parent dependency in children. At the end of the day, it's not a matter of if the children will leave the parents bed, which is what stops some people from co-sleeping; it's a matter of when. All children end up leaving their parents' bed, even when that decision is left up to them. However, parents need to be aware of the fact that there will be a loss of intimacy between them, which eventually might interfere in the couple's and family dynamics.

At the end of the day, it is your decision as a parent whether you want to co-sleep with your baby. Regardless of what you decide, there are general safety guidelines that you should take in to consideration that you can find below. In any case, try to have consistent day and night sleep conditions. I know that sometimes this is not possible, but to the extent possible, make sure your baby naps in his crib, in the darkness, with no noise. You want your baby's environment to be the same when he wakes up in the middle of the night as it was when he fell asleep.

Finally, don't let your baby sleep in car seat or stroller for a long time; and don't let your baby fall asleep on the sofa or untied on a swing or bouncy seat.

✎ *Safe Co-Sleeping*

As mentioned above, adult beds are not usually prepared for safe co-sleeping without making certain modifications. If you've made the decision to co-sleep with your baby, make sure you follow these safety guidelines:

- Always leave your child's head uncovered while sleeping.
- Make sure your bed's headboard and footboard don't have openings or cutouts that could trap your baby's head.
- Make sure your mattress fits snugly in the bed frame so that your baby won't become trapped in between the frame and the mattress.
- Don't place a baby to sleep in an adult bed alone.
- Don't use pillows, comforters, quilts, and other soft or plush items on the bed.
- Don't drink alcohol or use medications or drugs that may keep you from waking and may cause you to roll over onto, and therefore suffocate, your baby.
- Don't place your bed near draperies or blinds where your child could be strangled by cords.

The crib is the only place where you leave your baby on his own, therefore you should make sure it's 100% safe and soothing. Do not use your child's crib for time-outs, to control tantrums, or for disciplining. Bedtime needs to be a secure, loving time, not a punishment. Therefore, never use sending your child to sleep as a threat. You want your child to have a positive association with his crib. I will talk about when it is the right time to transfer your baby from the crib to a toddler bed in Chapter eight: Smooth Baby Sleep Approach/ Step 4: Apply Age by Age Considerations.

Empty Crib

Only your baby should be in the crib, on the mattress, to reduce the risk of suffocation, strangulation, or harm to your baby; and make sure your baby associates the crib with sleep, not with active play.

The mattress should be firm, fitting tightly to the crib without any gaps on the sides, and it should only be covered with a tight sheet. More babies die every year from suffocation in plush sleeping environments than from defective cribs. Here's the breakdown of things I do not recommend you to have on your baby's crib:

- **No Bedding or Objects**
  Bedding such as pillows, thick quilts, comforters, pillows, sheets, stuffed animals, and blankets pose a suffocation hazards. To keep your baby warm, try a sleep sack or other sleep clothing that doesn't require additional covers. If you use a blanket, make it lightweight. Tuck the blanket securely at the foot of the crib, with just enough length to

cover your baby's shoulders. Then place your baby in the crib, near the foot, covered loosely with the blanket. Don't cover your baby's head.

- **Bumpers**

  Many infants lack the motor development needed to free themselves when they become wedged between the bumper and another surface. If the bumper pads are too soft and cushiony, your baby's nose or face can get pushed up against it, and she could suffocate. If they are too firm, your baby can use them as a stepping-stone, climb up on them, and jump out of the crib.

- **Sleep Positioners**

  They can carry the risk of suffocation and death. If you're using sleep positioners with your baby, stop using them; the modest benefit does not outweigh the risk. Health officials say the mats with barriers designed to prevent a baby from rolling over shouldn't be used under any circumstances.

- **Toys**

  I normally do not recommend having any toys or books inside the crib, not only because they can pose suffocation hazards or injuries, but also because they might get your child too excited and transform your child's crib into a play zone. This could confuse your child and prevent him from establishing the right associations with sleep and with his crib.

- **Drinks and Food**

  Don't put your baby to sleep with a bottle of water, juice, or milk or with food. If juice, milk, or food is left in a baby's mouth for too long, it can cause tooth decay.

- **Mobiles**

  I do not have a problem with you having a mobile in your baby's crib during his first months of life, as long as you don't use it as a sleep crutch to get your child to sleep; as that would go against the goal of helping your child become an independent sleeper. As your child grows up, he can pull on the mobile, drop it on top of himself, and get hurt. Later on, he might use it as a stepping-stone to get out of the crib. Therefore, the use of mobiles up to 4 months is acceptable; anytime after that, it isn't recommended.

You can introduce a lovey, safety blanket, or a sleeping buddy at around 6-8 months but not before, due to risks of suffocation. See the box below for further information on introducing a safe lovey.

Introducing a Lovey or Sleeping Buddy

A lovey, safety blanket, or sleeping buddy can help your baby feel safe when you are not with her, and it can serve as a sleep cue when introduced during your sleep routines.

- Use it only at sleep times.
- Have it smell like you. Place it between your baby and you while you feed her, or wear it during the day so that it gets your scent.
- Make sure it's small enough for your baby to hold, but not so big that could cover your baby's face.
- Guarantee that it is safe. Make sure that it doesn't have removable pieces (hair, clothes, buttons, noses, Velcro, etc.) that your child could potentially choke on.

When the baby gets attached to her lovey, make sure you buy 2-4 of them so that you have a replacement in case it gets lost, or you have to wash it.

Your child's lovey might be the same throughout his childhood. However, don't be surprised if he grows out of one as the months go by and he gets attached to a new one every once in a while.

For a list of Smooth Parenting Approved loveys, and other product reviews, visit our website www.SmoothParenting.com.

Certified Crib

Make sure your child's crib is completely safe by making sure it follows the safety guidelines established by the Consumer Product Safety Commission (CPSC) website and Juvenile Products Manufacturers Association (JPMA). Beginning June 28, 2011, all cribs manufactured and sold (including resale) must comply with new and improved federal safety standards. The new rules prohibit the manufacturing or sale of traditional drop-side rail cribs, require strengthened crib slats and mattress supports, improve the quality of hardware, and require more rigorous testing.

Periodically check the list of recalled cribs on the CPSC website (www.cpsc.gov), and make sure your child's crib is not there. If it is, follow the recall steps that they suggest.

Use the crib (and all your baby's products) in the exact way the manufacturer details in the crib's manual. Follow the instructions provided and make sure that every part is installed correctly, as proper assembly of cribs is vital to your child's safety.

Check the crib frequently to make sure that all hardware (screws, bolts, springs, etc.) is secured tightly and that there are no loose, missing, or broken parts. With the mattress out of the crib, shake the crib to see how tight all the joints are. If the crib feels loose, shaky, or structurally not sound, tighten all hardware. If the crib remains unstable after tightening, look for loose wood-to-wood joints that may be the source of the problem. Stop using the crib if loose wood-to-wood joints are found.

Please, do not try to fix broken cribs; do-it-yourself crib repair is always dangerous and could turn out deadly. Your child is worth more than that. Worst case scenario, if you have to get rid of the crib to have it fixed, have no resources to buy a new one, and have no temporary solution (travel crib, pack and play, etc.) put the crib mattress to the floor and have your baby sleep on it.

Every time you change the sheets, make sure that there are no gaps larger than two fingers between the sides of the crib and the mattress.

Say 'No' to Drop Side Cribs; They Can Be Deadly

Drop-side cribs are those that have a side rail that moves up and down, allowing parents to more easily lift their child from the crib.

They have been found to be the cause of the deaths of at least 32 infants and toddlers since 2000, and they are suspected in another 14 infant fatalities. From 2005 to 2010, more than 9 million drop-side cribs have been recalled, including cribs from big-name companies such as Evenflo, Delta Enterprise Corp., and Pottery Barn Kids.

In 2010, the government outlawed drop-side cribs, banning their manufacture, sale, and resale. Note that a drop-side crib, even with an immobilizer installed, will not meet the new CPSC crib standards.

Therefore, if your baby is currently sleeping in a drop-side crib, I urge you to **get rid of it right now and buy a new, safe one**. Do not donate it to charity or pass it on to a neighbor or family member. If it's dangerous for your child, it's dangerous for everybody else's.

Safe Crib Surroundings

Inspect the area around the crib for potential hazards in case your baby decides to jump out of the crib. Never place a crib near a window with blinds, curtain cords, or baby monitor cords. They pose strangulation hazards. Finally, don't leave your unattended pet with access to your sleeping baby.

5. Everyone on Board

Caregivers and Support

You need to list everyone who is or will be involved with your baby and his care. Make sure everyone is informed about your child's Smooth Sleep Plan. This list might include nannies, babysitters, older siblings, grandparents, aunts, uncles, and friends. This is usually an overlooked part of the plan that is essential for the plan to work. Everyone should know the plan and follow it in the same way so that your child doesn't get confused.

Pediatrician

It is prudent to discuss any of your concerns about sleep issues with your child's pediatrician before you start any sleep-training program. Ask the following questions:

- Is your baby gaining weight regularly?

- Are there any other medical problems that might be causing your baby's sleep problems?

- Are there any developmental conditions affecting sleep?

- Is there any reason why you shouldn't go ahead with sleep training?

- Is there any sleep training method that is not advisable for your baby?

Your pediatrician knows your baby and watched him grow and develop week by week. Therefore, she will be able to assess whether your child is ready to begin formal sleep training. I actually require the families I work with obtain approval to begin the Smooth Baby Sleep program from their pediatrician when their baby is around 12 weeks of age. This ensures that your baby is developmentally ready to begin the process of sleep training and that no medical issues will impede the process.

DESIGN YOUR CHILD'S TAILORED SCHEDULE

"We first make our habits and then, our habits make us."
- JOHN DRYDEN

The Importance of a Tailored Schedule

Children do develop better, grow better, and behave better when they know what to expect from their days, when a routine (this doesn't mean it has to be boring!) is in place for them to follow. Additionally, once they have a set schedule, parents will be able to better plan and organize their day and will be able to get more things done for themselves.

The schedule should be completely tailored to your baby's natural cycles and rhythms, and this will guarantee that he has a healthy sleep. Therefore, the first step towards building your child's tailored schedule is to "learn" your baby; and the second step is to analyze how healthy or unhealthy his sleep is so that we can build a schedule that targets his specific sleep challenges and deficiencies.

The result of implementing a good schedule that works for you and your child will be a more peaceful, less chaotic, and more

91

harmonious home. There, you and your children will be able to thrive as individuals and as members of a family unit.

Having the right schedule in place is 70% of your baby's sleep success. In fact, the first assignment that I always give the families I work with is to implement their child's tailored schedule that I've prepared for them. After 2 to 5 days in the new schedule, we start sleep training. In many cases, implementing the new schedule solves the child's sleep problems, as her problems were only caused because her current schedule wasn't working for her. So, even if you end up not doing any sleep training, make sure you have the perfect schedule for your child in place.

The main steps that we are going to follow when designing your child's fully customized schedule are listed below and are explained step by step after Jake's story.

1. "Learn" your baby: Daily Logs

2. Review daily logs and summarize key findings

3. Find the gap: Your child's sleep health diagnosis

4. Apply the scheduling guidelines

5. Put it all together: Your child's tailored schedule

❧ Jake, 14 Months Old

"We had been struggling with our son Jake's sleep for 14 months. My husband and I took turns—one of us would spend the night with him, and the other one would sleep. Truth be told, nobody was sleeping properly, and the worst part was that Jake wasn't happy. He was absolutely sleep deprived, and he didn't know what to do with himself.

Friends, family, and Jake's pediatrician told us many times that we had to leave him to cry himself to sleep. We were horrified at the idea, but we were so desperate that we tried. Jake screamed for hours every night. After one week, we had seen no improvement. To the contrary, now our son was scared to even get in his room.

At that point, we heard about Smooth Parenting, and hesitantly, we contacted Diana. She analyzed our son's sleep diaries and designed a customized schedule for our son that had nothing to do with the schedule that we initially had.

We started implementing it, and to our surprise, our son was happily sleeping more hours than ever after just 4 days. We were astounded! We hadn't even started sleep training yet. Not one of the days that we followed the schedule did Jake cry himself to sleep. By day 7, Jake was sleeping on his own. He was happy during the day, full of life, and excited about doing things.

We never truly believed Diana when she said that having the right schedule in place makes a tremendous difference, until we experienced it with our son. Yes, we did have to make compromises, and we had to change our own schedules a little bit. But it was so worth it!"

Anna & Simon Spencer
Parents to Jake, 14 months old
Omaha, NE

1. "Learn" Your Baby: Daily Logs

"The trouble with learning to parent on the job is that your child is the teacher."

- ROBERT BRAULT

The first step to figure out your child's optimal schedule, and one of the first and best things that you should do as a new parent, is to learn your baby. The best way to know your baby is being "plugged in" while you're with her. Pay attention to the way she communicates with you. **The purpose of logging your baby daily during the first 2-4 months is to "learn her."** You want to learn her "language" and be able to understand how she signals when she's hungry, tired, overwhelmed, overly tired, etc. You want to understand how her internal body clock works. (Revisit Chapter Six: How Sleep Works, for further information of internal body clocks.) You want to learn what calms her, what soothes her, and what makes her anxious. You want to learn what the best sleep routine is for your baby and for yourself.

Common baby's hunger cues are: mouth movement, sucking, rooting, crying, fussing, and frantic head movements. Common baby's sleepiness cues are: rubbing eyes, yawning, staring, crying, fussing, alertness, and whining. **But, remember, each baby is different, so your baby will have his/her own cues.** As long as you learn and follow your baby's cues and respond accordingly, he will develop healthy eating and sleeping habits on his own.

The purpose of logging your baby after those first 2-4 months is to be able to create a schedule that works for your baby. So, if your baby is over 2-4 months and her schedule is hectic, and her sleep habits aren't the healthiest, the first step towards better sleep is tracking your baby. Pick a week and start tracking. Let your baby lead the schedule a little bit more that week. This way, you will know what her natural waking times, napping times, feeding times, and bedtimes are. You will learn his cues and signals, and you will be able to build a completely customized schedule that will work perfectly for your child from there on. You need to track these four things: mood and cues, sleep time, feeding time, and diapering.

Keeping a daily log will help you have a better idea on what is really going on with your child's sleep and how far your child is from having the healthy sleep she needs and deserves. I often hear from the families that I work with how eye opening the process of tracking their babies and writing it down has been.

I will show you the steps of designing a customized schedule, as I walk you through how I designed baby Abigail's schedule. She was 5.5 months old at the time. The table below is a sample of a daily log of hers:

Time	Sleeping	Mood	Feeding	Diapering
6:00am	Woke Up	Cheerful	8oz milk	Pee
6:30am		Cheerful	Rice cereal	
7:00am		Ok		Poop
7:30am		Ok		
8:00am		Ok		
8:30am		Tired		
9:00am	Nap			Pee
9:30am	Nap			
10:00am	Nap			
10:30am	Woke Up	Cheerful		Pee
11:00am		Ok		
11:30am		Whining	8oz + Oatmeal	
12:00pm		Crying		Poop
12:30pm		Whining		
1:00pm		Crying		

1:30pm		Whining		Pee
2:00pm		Crying	8oz bottle	
2:30pm		Clingy		
3:00pm	Nap			
3:30pm	Nap			
4:00pm				Pee

Figure 4: Abigail's Daily Log – Day 1

Note: This example only shows the daily log from 6am to 4pm. However, each log should include 24 hours, in fact this particular one goes from 6am to 6am the next day.

You can find a template of the daily log at the back of this book, in the Appendix; or you can download it from the website for a more convenient use. Visit the book's readers' website at www.SmoothBabySleepBook.com. Once there, click on the "Templates & Trackers" section and introduce the code SBSBOOK.

2. Review Daily Logs and Summarize Key Findings

Once you have tracked your baby for 5-7 days, you can compare each day, column by column, and you will find a sleep-awake pattern. That's your child's natural cycle! In the example below, you can see how I combined and analyzed baby Abigail's daily logs information to figure out what her natural sleep-awake cycles are.

Time	Day 1	Day 2	Day 3	Day 4	Day 5	Day 6
6:00am	Sleep	Sleep	Sleep	Sleep	Sleep	Sleep
6:30am	Up	Up	Up	Sleep	Up	Up
7:00am				Up		
7:30am						
8:00am						
8:30am						
9:00am	Nap		Nap	Nap		Nap
9:30am	Nap		Nap	Nap	Nap	Nap
10:00am	Nap	Nap	Nap	Up	Nap	Nap
10:30am	Up	Up	Up		Up	Up
11:00am						

Figure 5: Abigail's Side-by-Side Analysis - Sleep

Note: This example only shows the daily log from 6am to 11am. However, each log should include 24 hours.

The most important two pieces of information that you can obtain from this analysis is when your baby's natural waking time is and what his sleep signs are. These are instrumental to build your child's schedule around. During this exercise, you might find out that your baby's natural waking time or bedtime is earlier or later than you initially thought. In baby Abigail's example, you can see that her natural waking time was 6am. This is going to be the first input to your child's schedule.

By analyzing this table side by side, with your baby's daily mood, you will learn how your baby is signaling you when she's ready to go to sleep, when she is overly tired or when she is ready to play. See Abigail's example below:

Time	Day 1	Day 2	Day 3	Day 4	Day 5	Day 6
6:00am	Sleep	Sleep	Sleep	Sleep	Sleep	Sleep
6:30am	Happy	Happy	Happy	Sleep	Calm	Happy
7:00am				Happy		
7:30am						
8:00am	Calm, Lack of Focus	Quiet	Calm, Tired		Calm, Giggly	Calm, Lack of Focus
8:30am	Crying, Cranky	Crying, Cranky	Fussing	Calm, Lack of focus	Crying, Cranky	Fussing, Crying
9:00am	Nap	Crying, Cranky	Nap	Nap	Crying, Cranky.	Nap
9:30am	Nap	Crying, Cranky. Fighting Sleep	Nap	Nap	Nap	Nap
10:00am	Nap	Nap	Nap		Nap	Nap
10:30am						

Figure 6: Abigail's Side-by-Side Analysis – Sleep and Mood

98

Note: This example only shows the daily log from 6am to 11am. However, each log should include 24 hours. In fact, this particular one goes from 6am to 6am the next day.

After reviewing Abigail's logs, we realized that when she became calm, lost focus, or seemed to quiet, she was signaling that it was time for her to sleep. You can see that when she was put to sleep after signaling that, she would peacefully go to sleep (see days 1 and 4). However, when she wasn't put to sleep then, Abigail would get cranky, start crying and fussing, and would fight sleep (see days 3 and 6). Additionally, when her mom waited too long, Abigail would start crying even harder; she would fight sleep; it would take her much longer to fall asleep; and she would sleep less (see days 2 and 5).

By utilizing these pieces of information (natural waking time, natural bedtime, and your baby's sleep cues), when building your child's schedule, you guarantee that you put your baby to sleep at the right time for him, which is Component 3 of Healthy Baby Sleep. Go back to chapter seven to review the components of healthy sleep if necessary.

3. Find the Gap: Your Child's Sleep Health Diagnosis

So far, you know what your child's natural cycle looks like and how his internal clock works, and you have also learned how your baby communicates with you. The last two pieces of information that you obtain from the daily logs will be used to analyze whether your baby is sleeping the right number of hours (Component 1 of Healthy Baby Sleep), with the right consolidation (Component 2 of Healthy Baby Sleep). That way, you will know whether your child is sleep deprived and what the main problems are that you are trying to solve when sleep training him.

Number of Hours

One of the first steps is always to make sure you know how much daytime and nighttime sleep your baby needs. Please go back to the tables that I shared with you before in Chapter Seven: Healthy Sleep, and that you will see again below, and check the right numbers for your child.

Age	Sleep Needs		
	Day (Hours)	Night (Hours)	Total (Hours)
0 – 2 Month	5 – 7	10 – 13	15 – 18
3 – 4 Months	4 – 5	10 – 12	14 – 16
5 – 6 Months	**4 – 5**	**10 – 12**	**14 – 16**
7 – 9 Months	2 – 4	11 – 13	13 – 15
10 – 12 Months	2 – 4	11 – 13	13 – 15
13 – 14 Months	2 – 3	11 – 13	13 – 15
15 – 18 Months	2 – 3	11 – 13	13 – 15
19 – 24 Months	2 – 3	10 – 13	12 – 15
2 – 3 Years	1 – 3	10 – 12	11 – 14
3 – 5 Years	0 – 2	10 – 12	11 – 13
5 – 11 Years	0	9 – 12	9 – 12
12 – 17 Years	0	8 – 11	8 – 11

Figure 7: Children's Sleep Needs by Age: Daytime and Nighttime Hours

Age	Day (Hours)	Number of Naps
0 – 2 Month	5 – 7	Several
3 – 4 Months	4 – 5	4 – 3
5 – 6 Months	**4 – 5**	**3 – 2**
7 – 9 Months	2 – 4	2
10 – 12 Months	2 – 4	2
13 – 14 Months	2 – 3	2
15 – 18 Months	2 – 3	2 – 1
19 – 24 Months	2 – 3	1
2 – 3 Years	1 – 3	1
3 – 5 Years	0 – 2	1 – 0
5 – 11 Years	0	0
12 – 17 Years	0	0

Figure 8: Children's Sleep Needs by Age. Daytime Sleep

Below, you can see an example of the daily log conclusions I obtained for baby Abigail, who, as I mentioned before, was 5.5 months old at the time.

101

Days	Day (Hours)	Night (Hours)	TOTAL (Hours)
Day 1	3.5	9	12.5
Day 2	2	8.5	10.5
Day 3	2	10	12
Day 4	2.5	9	11.5
Day 5	1	9.5	10.5
Average	2	9	11.5
5 – 6 Months	4 – 5	10 – 12	14 – 16
GAP	-2, – 3	-1, -3	-2.5, -4.5

Figure 9: Abigail's Healthy Sleep Assessment – Component 1: Number of Hours – Total Sleep

As you can see in the table, Abigail was clearly sleep deprived. She was sleeping 2 to 3 hours less than what she needed during the day; and 1 to 2 hours less during the night.

Consolidation

You also want to know whether your child is having the right sleep consolidation. In order to figure that out, you need to combine that information from the daily logs, and answer the following questions:

> Did he wake up in the middle of the nap? If so, after how many minutes? How long was he awake?

> Did he wake up during the night? If so, how many times? When did those wakings happen? How long was he awake? What was his longest sleeping stretch?

Age	Night Sleep			TOTAL (Hours)
	Night (Hours)	Bedtime: Hours Since Last Nap	Sleeping Through the Night: Longest Stretch Without Waking (Number of Wakings)	
0 – 2 Month	10 – 13	Varies	2.5 – 4 (many)	15 – 18
3 – 4 Months	10 – 12	2 – 2.5	4 – 8 (2 – 4)	14 – 16
5 – 6 Months	**10 – 12**	**2 – 3**	**6 – 12 (0 –2)**	**14 – 16**
7 – 9 Months	11 – 13	3 – 5	8 – 13 (0- 1)	13 – 15
10 – 12 Months	11 – 13	3.5 – 5	8 – 13 (0- 1)	13 – 15
13 – 14 Months	11 – 13	4 – 5	11 – 13	13 – 15
15 – 18 Months	11 – 13	4 – 5	11 – 13	13 – 15
19 – 24 Months	10 – 13	4 – 5	10 – 13	12 – 15
2 – 3 Years	10 – 12	4 – 6	10 – 12	11 – 14
3 – 5 Years	10 – 12	11 – 14	10 – 12	11 – 13
5 – 11 Years	9 – 12	12 – 13	9 – 12	9 – 12
12 – 17 Years	8 – 11	13 – 16	8 – 11	8 – 11

Figure 10: Sleep Needs by Age, with "Sleeping Through the Night" Guidelines

For an easier view of this information, you can go to the Appendix and review the summary table "Children's Sleep Needs by Age" table, which combines the information from all these tables. You can also download it from the website www.SmoothBabySleepBook.com. Once there, click on the "Reference Tables & Guidelines" section and introduce the code SBSBOOK.

The charts below reflect Abigail's daily log summary. She was waking up sometimes during her naps, but those wakings were very short. However, she was waking up an average of five times every night, which was considerably over the average among babies that age, which is 0-2. Additionally, her night wakings lasted an average of 13.5 minutes, which is too much.

Days	Day Sleep								
	Morning Nap			Mid-Day Nap			Afternoon Nap		
	Length	Wakings	Duration (minutes)	Length	Wakings	Duration (minutes)	Length	Wakings	Duration (minutes)
Day 1	1.5	0		0.5	1	2	1.5	3	2+2+2
Day 2	0.5	0		1.5	2	1+5			
Day 3	1.5	0		1	0		0.5	0	
Day 4	1	1	2	0.5	0		0.5	0	
Day 5	1.5	0		0.5	1	1			
Average	1	0	2	1	1	3	0.5	0	2
5 Months Old Needs	1-1.5	0		1-2.5	0		0.5-1	0	
GAP	0, -0.5	-		0, -1.5	+1		0, -0.5		
Conclusions	Short			Too short	Too Many				

Figure 11: Abigail's Healthy Sleep Assessment – Component 2: Consolidation – Daytime Sleep

Days	Night Sleep			
	Longest Stretch Without Waking	Night Wakings		
		Number	Duration of Wakings in Minutes	Total Awake Time
Day 1	2.5	5	2+10+15+10+12	49
Day 2	2	4	5+30+12+10	57
Day 3	2.2	4	2+3+10+20	36
Day 4	2.5	5	10+15+15+10+40	90
Day 5	3	6	15+3+45+10+5+15	93
Average	2.5	5	13.5	65
5 Months Old Needs	6 – 12	0 – 2		
GAP	-3.5, -9.5	+3, +5		
Conclusions	Poor Consolidation	Too Many		

Figure 12: Abigail's Healthy Sleep Assessment – Component 2: Consolidation – Nighttime Sleep

Throughout this section, you have seen many different tables summarizing my findings after analyzing Abigail's daily logs. However, I created all those individual tables for educational purposes and to explain to you every step of the process in a more clear way. In reality, I only use two tables, from which I pulled the information I shared with you above. Those two tables are shown below, and can also be found in the Appendix of this book.

1. "Comprehensive Daytime Sleep Assessment Table"

Days	Day (Hours)	Number of Naps	Morning Nap				Mid-Day Nap				Afternoon Nap			
			Hours since last sleep (waking)	Nap's Length	# Wakings	Wakings' Duration (Minutes)	Hours since last sleep (morning nap or waking)	Nap's Length	# Wakings	Wakings' Duration (Minutes)	Hours since last sleep (mid day nap or waking)	Nap's Length	# Wakings	Wakings' Duration (Minutes)
Day 1	3.5	3	2.5	1.5			2.5	0.5	1	2	2.5	1.5	3	2+2+2
Day 2	2	2	3.5	0.5			5	1.5	2	1 + 5				
Day 3	2	3	2.5	1.5			3	1			1	0.5		
Day 4	2.5	3	2	1	1	2	2.5	0.5			2.5	0.5		
Day 5	1	2	3	1			5	0.5	1	1				
Average	2	3	3	1	0	2	3.5	1	1	3	1.5	0.5	0	2
5 Months Old Needs	4 – 5	3 – 2	2 – 2.5	1 – 1.5	0		2 – 2.5	1 – 2.5	0		2 – 2.5	0.5 – 1	0	
GAP	-2, – 3	+1 – 0	+1, +0.5	0, -0.5	-		0, – 1.5	+1			0, – 0.5			
Conclusions	Not Enough		Too Late	Short			Too Late	Too short	Too Many		Too Early			

Figure: 13: Comprehensive Daytime Sleep Assessment

2. "Comprehensive Nighttime Sleep Assessment Table"

Days	Hours since last sleep (last nap)	Longest stretch without waking	Night Wakings		
			Number	Duration of Wakings in Minutes	Total Awake Time
Day 1	3	2.5	5	2+10+15+10+12	49
Day 2	4.5	2	4	5+30+12+10	57
Day 3	4	2.2	4	2+3+10+20	36
Day 4	4	2.5	5	10+15+15+10+40	90
Day 5	3.5	3	6	15+3+45+10+5+15	93
Average	4	2.5	5	13.5	65
5 Months Old Needs	2 – 3	6 – 12	0 – 2		
GAP	+2, + 1	-3.5, -9.5	+3, +5		
Conclusions	Too Late	Poor Consolidation	Too Many		

Figure: 14: Comprehensive Nighttime Sleep Assessment

In these two tables, I input all the necessary information, analyze it, and draw my conclusions from. As you can see in the images above, those tables have multiple columns and rows and are too big for a comfortable read here. You can find them in a bigger size in the Appendix of this book, and you can also go to www.SmoothBabySleepBook.com to download your copy for easier use. Once there, click on the "Templates & Trackers" section and introduce the code SBSBOOK.

Main Findings: Diagnosis

The main conclusions that I gathered from the above tables about Abigail's internal clock, symptoms, and sleep challenges were:

1. **Natural Waking Time: 6am**

This was the starting point in her customized schedule. I tailored her schedule to her natural cycles. Thus, I started with her natural waking time. With an early riser, I would do the same thing, but I would also design a "schedule shifting plan" to get him to a later waking time. See more about early rising in chapter nine.

2. **Sleep Cues**

This is how Abigail signals her sleep needs:

*   Sleep Cues: calm, lack of focus, quiet
*   Tiredness Signs: crying, crankiness
*   Overtiredness Signs: crying, crankiness, fighting sleep

I used all this information, combined with the naps' guidelines (see section below for further information) to come up with the optimal times for her naps.

3. **Unhealthy Sleep: Sleep Deprivation and Poor Sleep Consolidation**

Abigail, at 5.5 months of age, needed between 4 and 5 hours of sleep during the day (divided in 2 to 3 naps) and between 10 and 12 hours of sleep at night (with 0-2 feeding wakings during the night). This would have brought her to an expected night sleep consolidation of 6 to 12, totaling 14 to 16 hours of sleep in a 24-day. I had this in mind when designing her customized schedule.

I designed a schedule that would allow her to not be sleep deprived anymore and would meet her sleep needs. I would also use this information to design her night schedule, allowing for 2 night feedings, as she might need 0 to 2 at this age. However, she was used to having 4-6 every night. I didn't want her to have to quit cold turkey, go straight to zero, and be unhappy and hungry, so initially I wanted to give her the opportunity to have to night feedings.

4. Apply the Scheduling Guidelines

Even though every child is different, there are general scheduling guidelines that you should follow when working on your child's customized schedule.

Natural Waking Time

Wouldn't we all love that our children wake up at 8:30am every day? Or even better, wouldn't we all love to have our children wake up at 7am from Monday through Friday? Baby sleep doesn't really work that way. The truth is most babies wake up early. Babies who wake up between 5:30am and 6:30am cheerful, happy, refreshed, and ready to start their day are in fact naturally early risers. A waking time in that range can be a biologically appropriate wake-up time for a child of this age.

For more information on early rising, I invite you to go to chapter nine. Make sure you understand your child's natural waking time (see chapter above), and build your child's schedule around it.

Nap Guidelines

Many people think that getting rid of naps, and having a late bedtime will help your baby sleep more and better. It's actually the opposite. The more they sleep, the more they sleep. The less they sleep, the less they'll sleep. As we saw in chapters four and seven daytime sleep is as important for our children as nighttime sleep is. Therefore, naps must always be protected for as long as possible, and they should also be quality sleep, not only quantity. To the extent possible, let your baby nap in a quiet, dark place, at the same time every day, and follow your naptime routine. (More on setting up the best sleep environment in Chapter Eight/ Step 1: Establish a Good Foundation).

The following table summarizes again the recommended number of hours and number of naps by age, as seen in Chapter seven: Healthy Baby Sleep.

Age	Day (Hours)	Number of Naps
0 – 2 Month	5 – 7	Several
3 – 4 Months	4 – 5	3 – 4
5 – 6 Months	4 – 5	2 – 3
7 – 9 Months	2 – 4	2
10 – 12 Months	2 – 4	2
13 – 14 Months	2 – 3	2
15 – 18 Months	2 – 3	1 – 2
19 – 24 Months	2 – 3	1
2 – 3 Years	1 – 3	1
3 – 5 Years	0 – 2	0 – 1
5 – 11 Years	0	0
12 – 17 Years	0	0

Figure 15: Children's Sleep Needs by Age- Daytime Sleep

Now that you've learned how many hours your child should sleep during the day and how many naps that would entail, we need to know how and when those transitions (from catnaps to naps, from 3 naps to 2 naps...) happen. The first two months of your baby's life, naps are very irregular and short. Around 2-3 months of age, she will settle on three naps per day (morning, mid-day, and afternoon).

As a general guideline, the **afternoon nap should be the shortest**, as it is the closest to bedtime and will be the first one to be dropped. If you let your child sleep too much in this nap, she will most likely have problems falling asleep and staying asleep. The **mid-day nap should be the longest** and placed around the middle of his waking day; this is the one that your child will maintain until her preschool years.

The first nap to be dropped, between 6-9 months of life, is the afternoon nap (3rd nap). The next nap to be dropped is the morning nap, around 15 to 18 months of age. And finally, your child will be dropping his last nap around 3 to 5 years of age.

Age	Morning Nap		Mid-Day Nap		Afternoon Nap	
	Gap*	Length	Gap*	Length	Gap*	Length
0 – 2 Month	Varies	Varies	Varies	Varies	Varies	Varies
3 – 4 Months	1.5 – 2	1 – 1.5	2 – 2.5	1 – 2.5	2 – 2.5	0.5 – 1
5 – 6 Months	2 – 2.5	1 – 1.5	2 – 2.5	1 – 2.5	2 – 2.5	0.5 – 1
7 – 9 Months	2 – 2.5	0.5 – 1.5	2.5 – 3	1.5 – 3	No Nap	
10 – 12 Months	2 – 3	0.5 – 1	2.5 – 3	1.5 – 3	No Nap	
13 – 14 Months	2 – 3	0.5 – 1*	2.5 – 5*	1 – 3	No Nap	
15 – 18 Months	No Nap		5 – 6	1.5 – 3	No Nap	
19 – 24 Months	No Nap		5 – 6	1.5 – 3	No Nap	
2 – 3 Years	No Nap		6 – 7	1 – 3	No Nap	
3 – 5 Years	No Nap		6 – 7*	1 – 2*	No Nap	
5 – 11 Years	No Nap		No Nap		No Nap	
12 – 17 Years	No Nap		No Nap		No Nap	

Figure 16: Children's Sleep Needs by Age - Nap Guidelines

The above table provides you with the general guidelines on naps. The columns titled Gap* refer to the gap of time between the last time your baby slept to the beginning of the next nap. Under the morning nap column, the Gap* column indicates the number of hours that passed since your baby woke up in the morning until the beginning of his morning nap. Under the mid-day nap column, the Gap* column indicates the number of hours that passed since your baby woke up from his morning nap (if he still has a morning nap) or from the time he woke up in morning (if he has already dropped his morning nap) until the beginning of his mid-day nap. Under the afternoon nap column, the Gap* column indicates the number of hours that passed since your baby woke up from his mid-day nap until the beginning of his afternoon nap.

✎ *Is your child ready to drop a nap?*

If your child is at an age where he might be dropping one nap, look out for the following signs to confirm whether she's ready to let go of that nap:

a) She consistently doesn't sleep for that nap at all, or is consistently sleeping 30 minutes or less in that nap
b) She doesn't seem tired enough for bed at night
c) She starts not sleeping well at night, waking up more frequently or waking up earlier in the morning

You will find more information in detail on when is the right time for dropping the naps and sample schedules for every age in Chapter Eight/ Step Four: Apply Age by Age.

Bedtime Guidelines

"The effects of delaying bedtime by even half an hour can be subtle and pernicious."

            - DR. WILLIAM C. DEMENT

✎ *What is considered bedtime?*

Most parents don't have a set bedtime during the first months of your child's life. In fact, many of the families I work with don't have a response to the question, "What is your child's bedtime?" Others call bedtime the time they go to sleep.

In order to start teaching your child the difference between day and night and to start establishing a healthy bedtime from the beginning, you should have a bedtime in your mind. **Your behavior from that moment on should change. It should be more relaxed with no more playing, should consist of soothing activities, and should take place in your child's nursery**.

As a general rule, I consider bedtime the time **12 hours after your child woke up in the morning** (his natural waking time). For example, if your child wakes up at 6:30am, his bedtime would be 6:30pm. This doesn't mean that your baby is going to be in bed by 6:30pm and won't wake up until 6:30am, especially not during the first months of life. In fact, during the first 2-4 months of life, your baby might intermittently awake from his bedtime until his next feeding (3 to 5 hours later).

So, why do I call that bedtime? Because I want to YOU to have that set time in your mind as your child's bedtime and I want you to change your behavior from that time on. This will help you and your child evolve his schedule as he grows older and develops more sleep consolidation.

If you and your child are used to having quiet time in his room, read a book, listen to music, cuddle, and relax after bedtime, since the beginning. When he is ready to sleep from that moment until his night feeding, the transition will be easy and smooth.

✥ *Early Bedtime*

Make sure you have an **early bedtime** in place. Don't fall into the trap of thinking that having a later bedtime is better, because your baby will be tired and sleep better. He will be overly tired, and that will backfire on you. He will take longer to fall asleep, and he will wake up more often at night. The best way to make sure your bedtime is early enough is to observe your child at around 4-5pm. If he's cranky and moody by then, bring your bedtime earlier.

One of the most common (and easy to solve) mistakes regarding baby sleep is having a bedtime that is too late for your baby. Here are some tips on **how to know whether your child's bedtime is too late**:

• **The Late Afternoon Test**

Look at how your baby is in the late afternoon. If she is cranky, sad, and whiny, your bedtime is too late! A well-rested child should be happy, playful, and in a good mood in the late afternoon. In the United States, I would consider 4pm-5pm late afternoons for a baby.

- **The Witching Hour Test**

  If your child consistently has a period of crankiness, clinginess, and fussiness at the end of the day (aka, Witching Hour) that means her bedtime is too late. Against popular belief, there is no reason why your child should be unhappy and uncomfortable on a daily basis.

- **The Sleep's Speed Test**

  It takes an average of 10 to 20 minutes for a healthy child to fall asleep. Experts argue that if your baby falls asleep as soon as her head hits the pillow, or if it takes her more than 20-30 minutes to fall asleep, on a daily basis; that means that she is probably sleep-deprived and an earlier bedtime is needed.

A good bedtime for most babies should be between 5:30pm and 7:30pm. If you're having trouble getting your baby to sleep at night, do the previous tests, and try bringing up her bedtime 15-30 minutes earlier. You won't believe the difference those 15 – 30 minutes can have on a child's sleep.

The following table gives you an indication of how many hours after your child's last nap that you should put him to sleep.

Age	Night Sleep		
	Night (Hours)	Bedtime: Hours Since Last Nap	Sleeping Through the Night: Longest Stretch Without Waking (Number of Wakings)
0 – 2 Month	10 – 13	Varies	2.5 – 4　(many)
3 – 4 Months	10 – 12	2 – 2.5	4 – 8　(2 – 4)
5 – 6 Months	10 – 12	2 – 3	6 – 12　(0 –2)
7 – 9 Months	11 – 13	3 – 5	8 – 13　(0- 1)
10 – 12 Months	11 – 13	3.5 – 5	8 – 13　(0- 1)
13 – 14 Months	11 – 13	4 – 5	11 – 13
15 – 18 Months	11 – 13	4 – 5	11 – 13
19 – 24 Months	10 – 13	4 – 5	10 – 13
2 – 3 Years	10 – 12	4 – 6	10 – 12
3 – 5 Years	10 – 12	11 – 14	10 – 12
5 – 11 Years	9 – 12	12 – 13	9 – 12
12 – 17 Years	8 – 11	13 – 16	8 – 11

Figure 17: Bedtime Guidelines

Note that this table was designed assuming that your child's naps are properly timed, as I explained in the previous section. In other words, if your child's naps are not properly timed, and for example, she is sleeping at 5pm for her last nap, following the table below would give you an extremely late bedtime, which would not work great with her internal clock and her natural waking time.

☙ Sophie, 6 Months Old

I recently worked with a family with a 6-month-old girl, Sophie. She wasn't napping well, she woke up many times in the middle of the night, and she took up to an hour to fall asleep every day. Kathy and Michael, the parents, had tried everything: crying-it-out, rocking her to sleep, co-sleeping, and more. They had great sleep routines in place, and the nursery was perfect. Still, Sophie wasn't sleeping properly, and her parents weren't sleeping either.

After analyzing Sophie's sleep logs, I realized that Kathy would keep Sophie awake until Michael arrived home from work so that he could see her before she went to bed. Michael arrived home between 6:45pm and 7pm, which wasn't "too late." Sophie's bedtime was 7:15pm. Michael and Kathy never thought that 7:15pm was too late—but it was. By keeping her awake until then, she became overtired which prevented her from falling asleep.

Sophie's sleep plan was one of the simplest ones I made, since initially I only changed her schedule, and it wasn't even a major change. I just moved Sophie's bedtime from 7:15pm to 6:00pm, and I adjusted the naps and daily schedule accordingly. Michael and Kathy thought I wasn't serious.

"I got so mad when Diana presented us with Sophie's customized sleep plan that I wanted to hang up the phone. We were already doing all the things in there, and the only recommendation was to tweak her schedule a little bit. I was expecting a full overhaul, since in my mind, we had already tried everything and nothing worked. I refused to believe that her late bedtime was the only reason for her sleep troubles,

I couldn't have been more wrong! To my surprise, the first day we followed Diana's schedule, Sophie didn't have her Witchy Hour! Her afternoon was happy and peaceful. That night, she fell asleep within 20 minutes, which was a major improvement. The second night, Sophie was sleeping within 10 minutes. She's been a fantastic sleeper ever since then.

I was amazed! Diana was right! Sophie's bedtime was the only cause for her sleep problems. Michael spends time with her before he goes to work, which is when Sophie is more active and happy anyways. Had we known that before, we would've made the change a long time ago!"

Kathy Braun,
Mother to Sophie, 6 Months Old
Edinburgh, United Kingdom

Your child's schedule should include all the pieces of the puzzle; it is not only about sleep. Her feedings should be appropriately timed so that she gets the amount of calories and nutrition she needs—as well as a healthy sleep. I am not a lactation consultant, pediatric nutritionist, or doctor. The following feeding guidelines are based on my research and experience working with hundreds of families. Please take these guidelines as that, and always review your sleep plan and schedule with your pediatrician.

As a general rule, from birth to 2 months of age, babies eat every 2 to 4 hours. As mentioned before, most babies do not need to feed at night by 4 to 6 months of age. Having said that, some might continue feeding until they are one year old, and others might stop when they are 3 months old.

AGE	WHAT?	DAY		NIGHT	
		Freq.	Number	Freq.	Num.
0 – 1 Months	Breast milk OR Formula	2 – 4	4 – 6	2 – 4	4 – 6
1 – 2 Month	Breast milk OR Formula	3 – 4	4 – 5	3 – 4	4 – 5
3 – 4 Months	Breast milk OR Formula	4	4	4 – 8	4 – 2
5 – 6 Months	Breast milk OR Formula	4	4	6 – 12	0 – 2
6 – 8 Months	Breast milk OR Formula	4	4		
	Solids (Cereal, Fruits, Veggies)	2 – 4	3		

AGE	WHAT?	DAY		NIGHT	
		Freq.	Number	Freq.	Num.
9 – 12 Months	Breast milk OR Formula	4	4		
	Solids (Add protein + Finger Foods)	2 – 4	3 + 2 Snacks		
13 – 18 Months	Breast Milk OR Whole Milk	2 - 4	3		
	Solids (Add nuts)	2 – 4	3 + 2 Snacks		
19 – 24 Months	Breast Milk OR Whole Milk	2 - 4	3		
	Solids	2 – 4	3 + 2 Snacks		
25 – 36 Months	Breast Milk OR 2% Milk	2 - 4	3		
	Solids	2 – 4	3 + 2 Snacks		

Figure 18: Feeding Guidelines

As you can see in the table below, breast milk, whenever possible, is enough to cover the nutritional needs of babies until they are six months of age. When breast milk is not an option, formula is an appropriate substitute. At 6 months of age, solids can be introduced (as long as the baby is ready), starting with cereal, fruits, and vegetables.

Solid food at this age is not offered from a nutritional point of view, for your baby is getting all the nutrients and vitamins he needs from the milk. Solid foods are introduced to help your child get used to new textures, new flavors, and a new way of eating. Therefore, during the first months of solid food, always offer the milk first, then the solids. Don't force food into your baby's mouth; let him explore the food and the spoon. He will soon start eating more and more solids. Follow his lead in this process. Once he is getting full meals with solids, he will naturally stop asking for and drinking less milk.

At 9 months of age, you can start introducing proteins and finger foods. At 12 months of age, you can offer whole cow's milk, and it'd be ideal to avoid bottles. Instead, substitute them for sippy cups or straw cups. At 18 – 24 months of age, your child may be ready to drink from an open cup.

In the Appendix of this book, you can find a table with the general feeding guidelines by age. You can also download that table online at www.SmoothBabySleepBook.com. Once there, click on the "Reference Tables & Guidelines" section and introduce the code SBSBOOK.

Breast is best... as long as it is best!

We have all heard about the "Breast Is Best" campaign, and I agree with it. **The benefits of breastfeeding are enormous**. Breast milk is the perfect nutrition for your child; even the best formulas are only imitations of breast milk. There are also proven health benefits for both mother and baby and obvious cost savings. Additionally, breastfeeding is one of the most joyful and special bonding experiences that you can have with your baby.

I always recommend that the families I work with try to exclusively breastfeed during the first six months of life of the baby. I recommend using breast milk over formula, even in special cases when babies can't breastfeed (i.e. premature babies). The mother can pump breast milk and offer it to the baby fresh and even keep a frozen milk supply for later on.

I, in fact, "breastfed" my twins until they were almost 8 months old (6 months adjusted age); however, those feedings weren't at my breast. After being born at 29 weeks, they had to spend over two months in the hospital. Despite many trials and many consults with lactation consultants, they were never able to properly feed at the breast. At some point, they could latch on and suck, but they were so weak that they got exhausted and didn't get enough milk. In addition, they both had severe gastrointestinal reflux (GERD) and would spit up often.

We were so concerned about their weight and development that I made the decision to avoid them the struggle of trying to breastfeed and burning all their energy trying. Instead, I continued pumping milk and offered it to them in a bottle. Was it easy for me? No, it wasn't. I had always wanted to breastfeed, and letting that go was not easy for me. Furthermore, pumping every 3 hours to maintain my milk supply to feed both babies wasn't easy or fun, but I am so glad I did it! My daughters' weight gain during their first year of life was fantastic. They were healthy and strong, and I am glad that I was able to do that for them.

Having said this, I understand that breastfeeding is not the right solution for everyone. Society has somehow stigmatized those who choose not to breastfeed. Do you remember the public health campaign comparing not breastfeeding with riding a mechanical bull while pregnant? It feels like women who choose not to breastfeed are egotistical, ignorant, or abusive. I think these types of messages are plain wrong and damaging, adding onto the self-imposed guilt and inadequacy most first time moms already feel.

There's no doubt in my mind that breast milk is better than formula—no doubt! But there's also no doubt my mind about the fact that breastfeeding is not for everyone. There are some medical conditions, such as HIV, AIDS, active untreated tuberculosis, maternal varicella virus, which is contracted two to four days prior to delivery or within six days of delivery, neonatal galactosemia, and human T-cell leukemia virus— all of these might make breastfeeding an undesirable option. Additionally, there are certain medications that nursing women might not take, and if they must, lactation might not take place. Always check with your health care provider before breastfeeding, if you have any of these medical conditions or if you are taking any medication.

Some women have jobs that are incompatible with nursing or pumping; and many of those can't afford or do not want to take longer maternity leaves (if any) or quit their jobs and stay home with their child.

"Breastfeeding is not always easy." I hear this every week from the women at the support groups for new moms that I attend every week. Many of them struggle with breastfeeding at first; they suffer from engorgement, sore and bleeding nipples, plugged breast ducts, or mastitis. As a result, their babies have

trouble latching on or sucking, and they keep losing weight. All these challenges add on to the current stress and anxieties that new moms already feel. The moms who successfully breastfeed, encourage those having trouble to try yet another lactation consultant, another nipple cream, another breast shield, another feeding routine, another nursing pillow, another nursing position… and to keep at it until they are successful. I agree, as long as the "keeping at it" doesn't interfere with their happiness and the way they parent their children.

I believe that happy babies come from happy moms, and I've seen so many moms absolutely miserable because breastfeeding is such a struggle. I don't think that's good for the mom or the baby. If breastfeeding becomes a terribly painful experience or filled with anguish and resentment (towards your body, yourself, or your child), then I would argue that bottle-feeding is the best option.

A lot has been said about the unique bond you develop with your child while breastfeeding. But that's only true when breastfeeding goes according to plan. If breastfeeding becomes a struggle, week after week after week, the mother will resent herself and her baby, and that will undoubtedly affect their bond. Additionally, I do believe that fathers can have a bond as special as the one that mother's have with their babies, even though they do not breastfeed. This is also true for adoptive parents and mothers who can't or choose not to breastfeed.

To sum up, I do believe that breast milk is a much better option than formula. I do believe that breastfeeding, when going well, helps create a unique bond between mother and child. Having said that, I do believe breastfeeding is not for everyone, and I do believe that mothers who can't or choose not to breastfeed can be just as good of mothers or better than some who chose to breastfeed.

❧ *Appropriate Activity*

Make sure your child has interesting, stimulating, age-appropriate, and varied activities during the day, including physical activity and fresh air, so that she can burn up energy, exercise her body and mind, and be looking forward the wind down time during naps and night time.

❧ *Consistency*

We have said this many times. It is essential for your child to have a clear and consistent schedule. Her wake up time and bedtime should be the same every day, regardless of the circumstances (weekend, holidays, etc.). We don't expect you to have a set time (i.e., 7:14am), but you should have a clear window, 10 minutes give or take, and be consistent. Therefore, if their bedtime is 7pm, sometimes your child might go to bed at 6:50pm and others at 7:10pm, but that's the entire amount of wiggle room that you should allow.

❧ *Flexibility: Grows with Your Baby*

I know it might sound contradictory, but realize that your baby will change enormously over the first year of his life. Realize that your baby will change enormously over the first months of his life, so your initial schedule will evolve into a new schedule within the first month, then again after another month, and so on. This is due to several factors:

(1) Babies soon begin to stay awake longer;

(2) The amount of their feedings will increase, as the number of feedings decreases;

(3) Some feedings will be dropped;

(4) Sleep training will take place (sleeping through the night will come); and

(5) New foods will be introduced.

Between 6 and 12 months, it should be much more stable, and the changes to it would be minor (i.e., pushing bedtime 15 minutes earlier).

5. Put It All Together: Design Your Child's Tailored Schedule

This is where all the above information comes together and you build your child's customized schedule. Below you will see the step-by-step process that I followed to design baby Abigail's schedule:

1. **Waking Time:**
   That is her natural waking time: 6am

2. **Feeding:**
   This feeding could be just breastfeeding or bottle-feeding, or that combined with solids (oatmeal, cereal, or fruits). Since I know from the logs that Abigail was already starting to eat solids, I planned for it in her schedule. Some babies need a 30-minute break between their milk intake and their solids intake. At her age, it should be within the first hour after waking: 6:30am.

3. **Active Play**

4. **Morning Nap:**
   It should be 2 to 2.5 hours after waking up, as you can see in the Nap Guidelines table that I shared with you in the previous section. I noticed in her log that she was showing her sleep signs (quiet, calm, lack of focus) around 8am. Therefore, that was her natural nap time: 8am.
   As I shared with you in the Nap Guidelines as well, the morning nap lasts 1 to 1.5 hours among children Abigail's age. As she had been consistently sleeping one hour in the morning, I kept the length at that. Therefore, Abigail's morning nap ended at 9am.

5. **Active Play**

6. **Feeding:**

   I know from her log that she was already taking some solids, but it was just an introduction. Thus, she should always have her full bottle first as she starts eating more and more solids. In the Feeding Guidelines, you see that she needs to be fed 4 hours after her last feeding, which was at 6:30am, so her bottle-feeding time is 10:30am and solids at 11am.

7. **Mid-Day Nap:**

   It should be 2 to 2.5 hours after the end of her morning nap, as you can see in the Nap Guidelines table that I shared with you in the previous section. I've noticed in her log that she is showing her sleep signs (quiet, calm, lack of focus) around 11:15am to 11:45pm. Therefore, her mid-day nap should start at: 11:30am.

   As I shared with you in the Nap Guidelines as well, this nap lasts 1 to 2.5 hours among children Abigail's age. As she is sleep deprived, and I want her to lengthen this nap before dropping her afternoon nap, I have allocated 2 hours for this nap. Therefore Abigail's mid-day nap ends at 1:30pm.

8. **Feeding**:

   As we saw in the Feeding Guidelines, this feeding will evolve to a snack as she introduces more solid foods. This feeding takes place at 1:30pm.

9. **Play**

10. **Feeding**:

    As we saw in the Feeding Guidelines, this feeding will evolve into dinner, as she introduces more solid foods into her diet. This feeding takes place at 4:30pm.

11. **Calming Routine:**

    Abigail starts getting ready for bed. She will get a calming and soothing bath, followed by a soft massage, and get dressed for bed. This process will start at around 5:00pm.

12. **Feeding:**
    This feeding happens 4 hours after her full feeding (1:30pm), it's the last one of the day and should happen in her nursery with dimmed lights.
13. **Bedtime**

The end result is the following schedule, fully customized to baby Abigail's natural internal clock, her sleep signs, and her sleep needs (day and night).

Time	Activities
6:00am	**Waking Time**
6:00am	**Bottle**
6:30am	**Solids**
	Active Play
8 am – 9am	Morning Nap
	Active Play
10:30am	**Bottle**
11am	**Solids**
11:30am – 1:30pm	Mid-day Nap
1:30pm	**Bottle**
	Play
4:30pm	**Solids**
5:00pm	Bath + Massage + Pajamas
5:30pm	**Bottle**
6:00pm	Bedtime
6pm-6am	Sleep

Figure 19: Abigail's Schedule at 5 Months of Age

We have designed and launched a mobile application that you can download to your iPhone and iPad, to help you find the right schedule for your baby based on her natural cycles, so you don't have to go through this process on your own. You just need to input your child's natural waking time that you've just found out after your analysis, her age, and a couple more details, and the application will give you the right schedule for your baby. Not only that, as your baby grows, the schedule will "grow" with your baby; and will give you sleep tips and reminders on when it's time for your child to drop a nap, push back her bedtime, etc. Therefore, if you don't want to spend the time and energy to design your child's tailored schedule, I'd invite you to check our app "Baby Sleep & Schedule" on iTunes or on www.BabySleepApp.com.

Step Three

CHOOSE THE BEST SLEEP COACHING METHOD FOR YOUR CHILD

"When you are a mother, you are never really alone in your thoughts. A mother always has to think twice, once for herself and once for her child."

- SOPHIA LOREN

Now, into the real deal: sleep training. I strongly believe that **no two children are exactly alike**, and that is the main pillar of the Smooth Baby Sleep Approach. Every child is different, and every family is different. Additionally, parents all have different parenting approaches, and I have to honor those. I also know that happy parents equal happy children. Because of these important individual differences between children, **it's impossible to offer one sleep training strategy and one schedule that will work for everyone.**

Therefore, I believe that I have the responsibility to give you the information about all the methods out there, and let you choose, as a parent, which one would work best for your child and your family. **<u>Do you want to know the truth of all those methods?</u> None of them will work for every child, and none of them will work on their own.**

As a general rule, I will never advise you to follow "cry-it-out," and I will always encourage you to minimize tears, and try the least invasive, gentler approach first. Unfortunately, even though, my method is not "cry-it-out," and one of my goals is to minimize tears, some parents might experience a little bit of crying during the first days of sleep.

Some babies will respond to sleep training without crying, and some might need to express their dislike for the new "habits" by crying. As long as you continue reassuring your baby periodically, crying is not necessarily problem. Your baby can't come and tell you, *"I don't like this change mom; I really want you to continue nursing me to sleep (or rocking me to sleep). I prefer when you get me to sleep. I don't like having to self-soothe. I don't know how to put myself to sleep, and it's frustrating for me to even try. Why can't you continue doing it for me?"* Crying is the only way children have to express their discomfort, and changing habits makes them feel uncomfortable for a while. I believe that babies cry for a reason, but that reason might just be *"I don't like this change."*

There are many sleep training philosophies and advocates out there: Dr. Weissbluth and Suzy Giordano's Cry It Out, Dr. Ferber's Controlled Crying, Dr. Sears' Nighttime Parenting, Elizabeth Pantley's No-Cry Sleep Solution, Sleep Lady's Shuffle, Super Nanny's Modified Cry It Out... the list is endless.

As I mentioned previously, I believe that every child is different. I don't believe that there's a "one-size fits all" solution when it comes to baby sleep training; if there were, we would all just follow the same steps and all our children would be great sleepers. I truly believe that different methods work for different people; all of them have pros and cons. **The only method that I do not follow and do not recommend parents is 'cry it out,"** which basically implies leaving your baby awake in his crib and letting him cry until he falls asleep. In fact, with "cry-it-out" you are not advised to go back in the room until your child's waking time. It saddens me to hear from many of the parents that I work with that their pediatrician has recommended them to follow the 6pm to 6am schedule. This means that they are to put their baby in the crib at 6pm, leave the room, and not go back in until 6am.

In my opinion, the risks of following this method clearly outweigh its advantages. Prolonged cries in babies cause increased blood pressure in the brain and decreases oxygenation to the brain. Research shows that when babies are left to cry alone and unattended, they experience panic, stress, and anxiety. Their little bodies and brains are inundated with adrenaline and cortisol stress hormones. When developing brain tissue is exposed to these types of hormones for lengthy periods of time, the brain nerves will not appropriately connect with other nerves. Therefore, it is more than likely that babies who endure many nights of crying-it-out alone are suffering harmful neurological effects that may have permanent implications on the development of their brains.

Additionally, excessive crying results in an over-sensitiveness to stress, which can lead to abandonment feelings, fear of being alone, separation anxiety, and panic attacks. Dr. Michael Lewis presented research findings demonstrating that "the single most important influence of a child's intellectual development is the responsiveness of the mother to the cues of her baby." A child that is left to cry it out might question her parents' responsiveness and love and her own sense of safety and protection.

Among the other methods that I use with my clients, I have found three to have great success when applied at the right age with the right type of child for that method. These methods involve little or no crying, and these are the ones that I will explain to you step by step in this section. I will also let you know when they work better and when they won't work. Having said that, none of these methods might be suitable for your child, or the best solution for him might be a combination of a couple of these methods.

These are the three methods I will be covering in detail:

1. No Tears/ Back It Out

2. Side By Side

3. Periodic Comfort and Reassurance

These methods support the sleep goals that I mentioned in 'Step One: Establish a Good Foundation - Golden Pillars of Smooth Baby Sleep.' They are effective; they promote independent sleeping; they don't damage the baby; and they don't disrupt the bond and trust between parent and child. Be discriminating and mindful about using any of these or any other method to help your baby sleep. Weigh them in against your knowledge of your child, of yourself as a parent, and against your own intuition as a mother. If it doesn't feel right to you, don't do it.

No Tears/Back It Out

Is it really possible to teach your child to sleep through the night on his own without having him shed a tear? My answer to this question is "**It depends.**" For some babies it is, and for others it is not. I go back to one of my principles "no two children are alike," and what works with one might not work with other.

Who and When?

The No-Tears Approach to sleep training is by far the most customizable one. It is the method that I tend to recommend to attachment parents; to parents dealing with continuous night-nursing; to parents whose children only fall asleep at the breast or at the bottle; to parents who co-sleep and want to continue co-sleeping; and to parents who are unwilling to let their babies cry at all, but are willing to stick to a sleep plan for as long as it takes. Although effective for some children, these techniques usually take much longer to produce results. This technique is more effective with younger babies than it is with toddlers.

How?

By "no-tears" I mean "no-heavy-crying," although your baby might protest and fuss during the process. The general idea of this approach is to make the transition to independent sleeping very smooth, gentle, and progressive. You start with what your child's current situation is and what the ideal situation is. Then, you build a plan to decrease the amount of "assistance" that your child receives under the current situation to fall asleep or go back to sleep. You back out from what you currently do into a new way of helping your child to sleep that is less interventionist but just as gentle, if not more.

The way to structure this process so that you advance and get closer to your goal is by breaking down the process into different milestones that you would have to reach before you get to the final, ideal situation. Then, divide those milestones into steps or actions.

a. Current Situation

     i.   Milestone 1
    ii.   Milestone 2
   iii.   Milestone 3

b. Desired Situation

Each milestone is a step away from your current situation and a step towards your desired situation. It can be as short or long as you and your baby can handle without crying. It is essential that you think about each and every one of the steps and the associated actions to get there so that you don't go back once you start moving forward.

Once you start moving towards one milestone, you can't go back to the current situation or to a previous milestone. For example, if the first milestone is to stop nursing your child a couple of minutes before she falls asleep, once you've reached that milestone, there's no going back to nursing your child to sleep. Once you've reached a milestone, I would encourage you to stay an additional 2 to 3 days there, before you move on to the next milestone. Your child will determine the speed at which you move from one milestone to the next, as you will not advance, until your baby is comfortable.

Some children might get even more upset by these minor changes that you are adding to their "rituals" than they would if you changed everything at once. Some parents have decided to go for another method, two or three weeks into the No-Tears Approach, as they were not seeing significant improvement and their children (and they) were still sleep deprived. Others have been thrilled with the idea of teaching their baby to sleep at the baby's pace, without crying, and they have celebrated every step in the right direction.

Before you decide to implement this method, make sure you understand what this process entails and the time, effort, and commitment that you will need to make this work. Try to anticipate how your child is going to react to each minor change. Here is an example to illustrate how this approach works:

∽ Jill, 8 Months Old

Jill needed to be rocked to sleep every night. Cindy, her mother, was a single parent since the sudden passing of her husband, Joe, when Jill was just 2 months old. Cindy hadn't been there for Jill the weeks after Joe passed. When she was able to take care of Jill, she did everything that she could to bond with her child, and one of her rituals was rocking her to sleep.

Even though she shortly thereafter realized it wasn't the best idea for her, she was thrilled that she had been able to rekindle the bond and connection, and she didn't want to jeopardize it again. She knew that she wasn't going to be able to follow through with anything that involved Jill crying.

"I didn't have any feelings about letting her cry it out or sleep training before. I thought I would do whatever I needed to do to help her become a good sleeper. However, I was so traumatized by Joe's passing that I knew I couldn't handle any crying".

Cindy Spencer
Memphis, TN

This is the bridge that we needed to build for Jill and Cindy.

Current Situation:

Jill is rocked to sleep every night and every nap. After that, she sleeps in her crib in Cindy's bedroom.

Desired Situation:

Jill is put in her crib awake, and she falls asleep on her own.

Even though it might not look like it, the gap between those two scenarios is considerable. Therefore, we set up intermediate milestones.

Current Situation: Jill is rocked to sleep every night and every nap. After that, she sleeps in her crib in Cindy's bedroom.

- *Milestone 1: Jill is gently rocked to sleep every night and nap. Cindy's rocking slows down and the motions are not as vivid.*

- *Milestone 2: Jill is held to sleep, but not rocked.*

- *Milestone 3: Jill is held until she's very drowsy, but she is still awake when put in the crib. Cindy stays touching and patting Jill until she falls asleep.*

- *Milestone 4: Jill is held until she is drowsy. She is placed in her crib while still awake. Cindy stays by the crib touching Jill, but without moving her arm or patting her.*

- *Milestone 5: Jill is held until she's drowsy. She is placed in her crib while still awake. Cindy stays by the crib until Jill is asleep, but there's no more physical contact.*

- *Milestone 6: Jill is held until she's drowsy. She is placed in her crib while still awake. Cindy stays by the crib for a short period of time, and then leaves before Jill is asleep.*

Desired Situation: Jill is put in her crib awake, and she falls asleep on her own.

The first days, our goal was "Milestone 1," decreasing the intensity of the rocking. Did Jill like it? No, she didn't love it at first. She was used to being very actively rocked, and this slow pace wasn't her cup of tea. Therefore, during the first couple of nights, Cindy would alternate active rocking and slow rocking. Until eventually, she was just slowly rocking Jill until she fell asleep.

The first five days, it took Jill an average of 10 minutes more than usual to fall asleep. This meant that Cindy was rocking (in a different way, but rocking) Jill for almost 30 minutes instead of 20. Once Jill was used to the slowly rocking, Cindy focused on "Milestone 2." Cindy continued decreasing the intensity of movement night by night, until she was just holding Jill until she fell asleep. Once Jill was comfortable with the new ways again, Cindy focused on "Milestone 3."

The first six nights working on "Milestone 3" were not easy. Jill wasn't happy about being placed in her crib when she was still awake, and Cindy had to pick her up several times, go back to holding her until she was drowsy again, and try placing her in the crib again.

Did Jill cry? Not really. She protested several times when placed in the crib, but Cindy responded immediately so that the cry didn't escalate.

Was the process easy on Jill? It was tiring, but comforting. Cindy was spending more time trying to get Jill to sleep, and it required much more of her than it did when she started with simply rocking Jill to sleep for 20 minutes. However, Cindy kept her eyes on the prize. She wanted to help Jill become an independent sleeper, and she was determined to it.

Around the 7th night working on "Milestone 3," Jill stopped fussing when being placed in the crib, and would calmly stay there while Cindy patted her back until she fell asleep. Once Jill got used to this new way of falling asleep, Cindy moved on to "Milestone 4," which was very fast and uneventful. Within 3 days, she had completely stopped patting Jill; she just placed her hand over her back until she fell asleep.

Then, Cindy moved on to "Milestone 5." The first 3 to 4 nights, she alternated placing her hand on Jill's back until she was calmed, removing it, placing it again if she got upset, and removing it again until Jill fell asleep. The 5th night on "Milestone 5" was the 1st night that Jill fell asleep without being touched by Cindy. After a couple of nights, Cindy focused on "Milestone 6," which took less time and effort than anticipated. Finally, she was in her "Desired situation."

Did it take long? Yes, it did. This is not an overnight solution. It took 40 days to get to Cindy's desired situation. As I mentioned before, Jill already slept through the night, she just needed assistance falling asleep on her own. If your child has more than one sleep challenge, this process will be even longer; but, as you see, **it can work**.

Side by Side

Who and When?

The Side-by-Side Approach to sleep training is the one that I tend to recommend for children who can't fall asleep on their own; whose parents spend a long time getting them to bed every night; who suffer from separation anxiety or have bad sleep associations with their crib; and whose parents want to be there for their child and want a solution sooner rather than later. This technique is not to be used before your baby's fourth month of age, especially if she gets upset and cries.

Although effective for most children, these techniques might overexcite some children and get them more anxious or frustrated as they see their parents there but that they are not holding them. Most babies get very upset during the first days of this approach, so they make as much noise and complaining as possible to go back to the previous habits. Therefore, the first days are hard on the parents, because they normally see a level of crying and frustration that they rarely seen in their children.

Some parents say that, even though it's heartbreaking seeing their child so upset, they are glad they are inside the room, making sure their child is not being harmed and letting their child know she's not abandoned. Other parents say that they would rather leave the room, than stay there watching their baby cry and not being able to respond right away. Think about how your child would react and how you would react if put in this position before making a decision about whether this method is the right one for your family.

It usually takes less time than the No-Tears Approach to produce results. This technique is as effective with younger babies as it is with toddlers.

How?

As its name indicates, the parent stays side by side with the child. The general idea of this approach is to make the transition to independent sleeping and crib sleeping without leaving the child's side right away. You will stay in your child's bedroom until he falls asleep, increasing the distance between the two of you frequently. You should decide beforehand whether you are going to stand, sit on a chair, or sit on the floor, and set it up before you start. I always recommend to parents that they use a comfortable chair.

As you go through this process, keep your child's door as it will be it once she falls asleep and you leave the room. If you will close the door when he falls asleep and you leave the room, keep it closed while you stay with him on your chair.

This method requires much less customization than the previous one, as the parent response and the plan of action is the same, regardless of what the initial sleep challenge(s) is/are. These are the steps:

Phase 1: Sitting Close By & Physical Touch (Days One to Three)

1. Ten to twenty minutes before nap time or bedtime, bring your child to the nursery.
2. Before you start the soothing sleep routine, let her know that it is time to sleep now and that after your routine, you will stay there in the room with her until she falls asleep, but you will not pick her up.
3. Follow your daily sleep routine. This can mean changing diapers, putting comfy pajamas on, singing a lullaby, hugging, rocking for a little bit, reading a book... whatever you have decided that your bedtime routine would be.
4. Put her in the crib, saying comforting words (i.e., "I love you, time to sleep now..."). You can pat her back for half a minute to a minute.
5. Sit on your chair or on the floor, whichever you have decided. You can still pat her back or just let her touch your hand (some babies do not like to be stroked, but love to hold your hand). You can also "shh" her a little bit, but do not engage in any other conversation from this moment on. Do not say, "It's time to sleep," "go back to sleep," "mommy loves you"... we all fall into that trap. Our words per se don't reassure them, we do.

    If your child stands up in her crib, let her stand. She will eventually sit and lie, especially if you are sitting by the crib.
6. Stay there, until she falls asleep. Then, leave the room, but keep the chair where it is, as you might have to come back to it during the night.

If she wakes up in the middle of the night:

7. Go back to her room, calm her without picking her up for one to two minutes (you can "shh" her, pat her back, and lie her back down if she was standing).

8. Sit on the same position you sat before. You can still pat her back or just let her touch your hand (some babies do not like to be stroked, but love to hold your hand). You can also "shh" her a little bit, but do not engage in any other conversation from this moment on.

    If your child stands up in her crib, you can put her back down, let her stand. She will eventually sit and lie, especially if you are sitting by the crib.

9. Stay there, until she falls asleep. Then, leave the room, but keep the chair where it is, as you might have to come back to it during the night.

❧ *Phase 2: Sitting Close By, No More Physical Touch (Days Four to Six)*

1. Ten to twenty minutes before nap time or bedtime, bring your child to the nursery.
2. Before you start the soothing sleep routine, let her know that it is time to sleep now and that after your routine, you will stay there in the room with her until she falls asleep, but you will not pick her up.
3. Follow your daily sleep routine.
4. Put her in the crib, saying comforting words ("I love you, time to sleep now..."). You can pat her back for half a minute to a minute.
5. Sit on your chair, at the same spot and position you have used until now. Do not pat her or touch her from that point on. She can reach out and grab your shirt, your hair, your arm, or your hand. That is perfectly fine; do not take her hands off of you. Let her touch you or grab you if she desires to do so.

    You can also "shh" her a little bit, but do not engage in any other conversation from this moment on.

    If your child stands up in her crib, let her stand. She will eventually sit and lie, especially if you are sitting by the crib.

6. Stay there, until she falls asleep. Then, leave the room, but keep the chair where it is, as you might have to come back to it during the night.

If she wakes up in the middle of the night:

7. Go back to her room, calm her without picking her up for one to two minutes (you can "shh" her, pat her back, and lie her back down if she is standing).
8. Sit on the same position you sat before. You can also "shh" her a little bit, but do not engage in any other conversation from this moment on.
   If your child stands up in her crib, let her stand. She will eventually sit and lie, especially if you are sitting by the crib.
9. Stay there, until she falls asleep. Then, leave the room, but keep the chair where it is, as you might have to come back to it during the night.

✎ *Phase 3: Sitting Near By (Days Seven to Nine)*

1. Place your chair 2 to 3 feet away from your child's crib, and closer to the door.
2. Ten to twenty minutes before nap time or bedtime, bring your child to the nursery.
3. Before you start the soothing sleep routine, let her know that it is time to sleep now and that after your routine, you will stay there in the room with her until she falls asleep, sitting on that chair, but you will not pick her up.
4. Follow your daily sleep routine.
5. Put her in the crib, saying comforting words ("I love you, time to sleep now..."). You can pat her back for half a minute to a minute.
6. Sit on your chair. The same spot and position, you have used until now. There's no physical contact from now on. She might get frustrated about it, especially the first night.

You can also "shh" her a little bit, but do not engage in any other conversation from this moment on.

If your child stands up in her crib, let her stand. She will eventually sit and lie, especially if you are sitting by the crib.

7. Stay there until she falls asleep. Then, leave the room, but keep the chair where it is, as you might have to come back to it during the night.

If she wakes up in the middle of the night:

8. Go back to her room, calm her without picking her up for one to two minutes (you can "shh" her, pat her back, and lie her back down if she is standing).

9. Sit on the same position you sat before. You can also "shh" her a little bit, but do not engage in any other conversation from this moment on.

    If your child stands up in her crib, let her stand. She will eventually sit and lie.

10. Stay there, until she falls asleep. Then, leave the room, but keep the chair where it is, as you might have to come back to it during the night.

✏ *Phase 4: Sitting Farther Away (Day 10 – Until You Reach the Door)*

1. Place your chair another 2 to 3 feet away from your child's crib, and closer to the door. So, now you are 4 to 6 feet away from your child's crib.

2. Ten to twenty minutes before nap time or bedtime, bring your child to the nursery.

3. Before you start the soothing sleep routine, let her know that it is time to sleep now and that after your routine, you will stay there in the room with her until she falls asleep, sitting on that chair, but you will not pick her up.

146

4. Follow your daily sleep routine.

5. Put her in the crib, saying comforting words ("I love you, time to sleep now..."). You can pat her back for half a minute to a minute.

6. Sit on your chair in the same spot and position, you have used until now. There's no physical contact from now on. She might get frustrated about it, specially the first night.

   You can also "shh" her a little bit, but do not engage in any other conversation from this moment on.

   If your child stands up in her crib, let her stand. She will eventually sit and lie.

7. Stay there, until she falls asleep. Then, leave the room, but keep the chair where it is, as you might have to come back to it during the night.

If she wakes up in the middle of the night:

8. Go back to her room, calm her without picking her up for one to two minutes (you can "shh" her, pat her back, and lie her back down if she was standing).

9. Sit on the same position you sat before. You can also "shh" her a little bit, but do not engage in any other conversation from this moment on.

   If your child stands up in her crib, let her stand. She will eventually sit and lie.

10. Stay there, until she falls asleep. Then, leave the room, but keep the chair where it is, as you might have to come back to it during the night.

Every 3 nights, move your chair another 2 to 3 feet away from the crib and closer to the door, until you are by the door. The bigger your child's bedroom is, the longer this process will take. Once you reach the door, stay there for another three nights, until you move out.

After three nights sitting by your child's nursery's door, it is time to move your chair outside. Place the chair outside the door and show it to your child as you bring her to her room at bedtime. Tell her that you are going to be there even though she won't see you.

If you typically leave the door closed when your baby sleeps and have been closing it during the sleep training process you can either (1) close the door behind you the first night you sit outside; or (2) leave it a little bit open the first three nights you sit outside of her room, and then close it the following three nights.

The fourth night (or seventh night, if you decided to leave the door semi-closed for three nights—option (2) above), do not place any chair. Let your child know that you will be close by as she falls asleep. This step is especially important for toddlers, and it's not as important for babies.

Once you are at this point, you can go closer to your child's bedroom door, as silently as possible, and "shh" her again if she's protesting. This way, she knows that even though she can't see you and that there was no chair, you are still around. Make sure she doesn't hear you stepping closer to the door and going away.

❧ Elliot, 19 Months Old

"Our son Elliot was 19 months old when we started working with Diana. He was used to falling asleep on the couch while we watched TV. My husband would then, transfer him to his crib. He would wake up within an hour or two crying for us. I would go, stay with him, rock him, nurse him, and sing to him—all the tricks I could think of. When he fell asleep, I left the room only to find myself inside the room doing the same thing within another couple of hours. Eventually, at some point during the night, out of exhaustion, I would bring him to bed with us, even though co-sleeping was not what we wanted for our family.

I told Diana from the beginning that I didn't want to leave my son crying alone, I wanted to be there with him; and that I wanted him to be able to fall asleep without so much help from us. I was four months pregnant with my second child then, and I didn't think it would be possible to go on like this once the second baby was born. Diana gave us a great schedule for Elliot and recommended us to follow the side-by-side method to help him sleep on his own.

The first night was very hard. Elliot was frustrated because I wasn't picking him up, and I was just sitting there. I patted his back and tried to help him to calm himself down. As I was going through this process, I realized that the only reason why he was upset and he was expecting me to 'get him to sleep,' was because I had taught him that. For over 19 months I had taught him that he needed me, the TV, the milk… and many other things to fall asleep. I made a promise to my unborn child that night that I would never do this to her. I would do my best to teach her how to sleep on her own early on so that she wouldn't have to go through what Elliot was going through now.

To my amazement, Elliot only woke up once the first night of sleep training. I followed the process, and he was back to sleep within 6 minutes, which was a record for him. It would always take me, or my husband, over 15 minutes to get him to sleep when he woke up.

The following nights were not easy, but they were not as hard as the first one. After the fifth night, I think he understood what the plan was and that I wasn't backing down. He stopped fussing or moaning when I placed him in his crib.

Every time I moved the chair farther away from him, I was scared he was going to freak out, but he didn't. He went along with the process. Even the 15th night, when I sat outside of his bedroom for the first time, he was fine. He called for me when I closed the door. I simply "shh"-ed him from the outside, and he was calmed.

Had I known about Diana and her sleep training approach before, I wouldn't have waited 19 months to help Elliot sleep. Even though I was doing all the things I was doing to get him to sleep with my best intentions, I was only creating bad sleep habits. My son was sleep deprived; he was constantly waking up in the middle of the night, which made him feel tired during the day. Since we sleep trained him, he is more active during the day. He is happier. He is more alert, and he is not as clingy as he used to be."

Stephanie Goldstein
Spring Valley, NV

Periodic Comfort & Reassurance

The Regular Comfort & Reassurance to sleep training is the one that I tend to recommend for children who can't fall asleep on their own; who wake up often at night; who have poor sleep associations with their sleep; and whose parents want to see improvement as soon as possible without leaving their children to cry it out.

Although effective for most children, these techniques might overexcite some children and get them more anxious or frustrated as they see their parents there but that they are not holding them. Most babies get very upset during the first days of this approach, so they make as much noise and complaining as possible to go back to the previous habits. Therefore, the first days are hard on the parents, because they normally see a level of crying and frustration that they rarely seen in their children.

Some parents say that even though it's heartbreaking seeing their child so upset, they know their child is not being harmed, and they are glad they still can reassure their child every so often. Additionally, they are even happier when the whole family is sleeping well in a short amount of time. Other parents say that they would rather spend more time and decrease the amount of crying. Think about how your child would react and how you would react if put in this position, before making a decision about whether this method is the right one for your family.

It usually takes less time than the previous two methods to produce results; most babies are sleeping independently with no-crying whatsoever in less than 7 to 10 days. This technique is not to be used before your baby's sixth month of age. This technique is more effective with babies between 6 to 18 months of age. I wouldn't recommend it for toddlers over 2.5 to 3 years of age.

How?

This method requires much less customization than the 'No Tears/ Back Out' explained before, since the parent response and the plan of action are the same, regardless of what the initial sleep challenge(s) is/are. The general idea of this approach is to make the transition to independent sleeping by encouraging infants to learn to "self-soothe," and regularly reassuring them. You follow your bedtime routine, place your baby to sleep in her crib, and leave the room. If she starts crying, you need to wait for a certain amount of time. If the crying continues, then you can go back to check on her and to calm her for a short time. When you check on her, go directly to her crib and give her a soothing and calm reassuring pat, but do not prolong your stay in the room. You will defeat the purpose of sleep training if you stand there for too long patting her to sleep. You come back out, and you wait to check on her for a longer period of time. You repeat the process until your baby stops crying and is sleeping.

There is no magic rule about how often you should check on her, and you may have to experiment a bit and find intervals that you and your baby are comfortable with. If your intervals are too short, she may treat it like a game and get even more stimulated, or she may not get the idea that she is supposed to self-soothe. If your intervals are too long, she may get worked up and upset; she might feel abandoned; and she might be exposed to the same risks I mentioned with the "cry-it-out" method.

When I work with families in my private practice, I tend to follow the intervals below. However, I always discuss everything with the parents, and sometimes, I will adjust them to better tailor the child's needs and personality. It is essential that you time yourself during the process, or you will find yourself waiting too much or too little.

Age	1st Check In	2nd Check In	3rd Check In & Following
Children 6 to 12 Months of Age	3	6	12
Children 13 to 18 Months of Age	4	7	15
Children 19 Months and Older	5	8	18

Figure 20: Regular Comfort & Reassurance Intervals (In Minutes)

Below you can find the step-by-step guidelines explained in detail. Follow these same steps when he wakes up in the middle of the night or naps:

1. Ten to twenty minutes before nap time or bedtime, bring your child to the nursery.
2. Before you start the soothing sleep routine, let her know that it is time to sleep now and that after your routine, she will stay there in her crib, and you will leave. Make sure that she knows that you will stay nearby if she needs you.
3. Follow your daily sleep routine. This can mean, changing diapers, putting on comfy pajamas, singing a lullaby, hugging, rocking for a little bit, reading a book... whatever you have decided that your bedtime routine would be.
4. Put her in the crib, saying comforting words ("I love you, time to sleep now..."). You can pat her back for half a minute to a minute.
5. If she starts crying, wait for ["*first check-in*"] minutes to go in back again and reassure her. You can pat her back and "shh"

her, but do not pick her up for 30 to 60 seconds. This time, you can say again, *"Night, night. It's time to sleep."* Your goal is not to get her to sleep. You goal is to let her know that you are there if she really needs you, but it's time to sleep.

6. If she starts crying once you leave the room, wait [*"second check-in"*] minutes outside.

7. If after that time she is still crying, go inside and repeat Step 4, without talking this time. If she's not crying, or you feel she's calming down on her own, don't go inside. For example, if she's talking or making noises, fussing but not crying, don't go in; this may cause her to get worked up again.

8. If she starts crying again once you leave the room, wait [*"third check-in"*] minutes outside.

9. If after that time she is still crying, go inside and repeat Step 4, without talking this time. If she's not crying or you feel she's calming down on her own, don't go inside. For example, if she's talking or making noises, fussing but not crying, don't go in; this may cause her to get worked up again.

10. If she starts crying again once you leave the room, repeat Steps 8 and 9 until your baby is either calmed or sleeping.

☙ Charlotte, 9 Months Old

Charlotte didn't have a set bedtime routine. Sometimes she fell asleep in her parents' arms, sometimes in the stroller, sometimes in her swing (which was too small and unsafe for her already), and sometimes at the bottle. Charlotte woke up often during the night. The response of her parents, Padma and Jeffrey, wasn't consistent. Sometimes she was rocked back to sleep; sometimes she was strolled back to sleep; sometimes she was left to cry for different and unpredictable intervals; and sometimes she was brought to her parents' bed.

Regardless of what the first response was, she was usually helped back to sleep. Even when they left her to cry, they eventually went back and soothed her. The inconsistency was making her cry even more, since the lesson she had learned was "If I cry hard enough and long enough, my parents will come back and help me sleep."

The first night following the Regular Comfort & Reassurance method was hard on Charlotte and her parents. She was still thinking that if she cried, she would eventually be held, which wasn't the case. She cried the whole 3 minutes during the first check-in waiting time. Jeffrey went to check on her and came back out. Charlotte was still crying, and she cried for the next 6 minutes. Jeffrey went back to check on her again and came back out. Charlotte was still crying, although the intensity of the cry had considerably decreased. Charlotte slept after another 6 minutes, so Jeffrey didn't have to go check on her the third time.

During the night, Charlotte woke up twice. The first time, she cried for 3 minutes before Jeffrey went to check on her. When he left the room, she was just fussing, and within 2 minutes, she was back to sleep. The second time she woke up she cried for 3 minutes before

Jeffrey went to check on her, she continued crying for another 3 minutes, and then she fell back to sleep. This was a major improvement for them, as Charlotte was usually awake, crying and protesting, for at least 15 minutes when she woke up during the night before sleep training.

The next day, she had a hard time falling asleep for her morning nap. She was used to falling asleep being strolled, held, or fed. She cried on and off for approximately 20 minutes. Her second nap went more smoothly. She cried for less than 3 minutes and then slept for 1.5 hours—a record for her. Charlotte was used to catnap; her naps before sleep training were never longer than 45 minutes.

The second night, Charlotte seemed to understand the new process a little bit better. She still didn't like it, but she started to get the concept. She cried for 3 minutes before Padma went to check on her and came back out. Charlotte continued crying for another 6 minutes before Padma went in for the second time. Charlotte only cried for another minute after Padma came back out.

During the night, she woke up twice. The first time, Padma went to check on her after 3 minutes, and Charlotte was back to sleep within minutes after she came back out. The second time, Padma didn't have to go check on her, since Charlotte put herself back to sleep after 2 minutes. The next day, naps went much better as well.

The fourth night of sleep training, Charlotte seemed calmed and secured when she was placed in her crib at night, and it was the first night she didn't cry. It was also the first night that she didn't wake up during the night.

The fifth day of sleep training, Charlotte was also sleeping long, restorative naps, without crying.

"We were so desperate when we contacted Diana. The sleep deprivation was affecting our marriage, we were feeling resentment towards Charlotte; and needless to say, she was miserable and exhausted as well.

We couldn't believe that within less than a week following Diana's Smooth Baby Sleep Plan that she had become such a great sleeper. The schedule that she provided for us was right on, and the sleep training method worked out perfectly for our daughter and for us.

Now our daughter loves our bedtime routine, and she looks forward to bedtime. It has been a remarkable improvement for all of us as we feel better rested during the day; our fears of nighttime drama have gone away; and we don't take out our exhaustion on each other— because there is no more exhaustion. We highly recommend Diana and her sleep training methods."

Jeffrey & Padma Girard
Montreal, Canada

APPLY AGE-BY-AGE CONSIDERATIONS

"As a parent, the days are long but the years are short."
- Unknown Author

In this chapter, I will address specifics developmental milestones, sleep guidelines and parenting tips for every age group. Please remember, this information is provided as a general guide only. Every child is different, and certain developmental milestones, physical limitations, and family-related circumstances might influence the amount of sleep your child needs.

Expectant Parents

I know it might look peculiar that I have added a chapter for expectant parents when most books about baby sleep and sleep training usually start when the baby is born or after the twelfth week of life. Against common knowledge, there are 4 things you can do while you are pregnant that will directly affect the way your baby sleep develops.

1. Learn to prioritize sleep. Sleeping is as important as feeding, not only for your baby, but for you as well.

2. Set up the best possible nursery for your baby, which is safe and sleep conducive. Go over Chapter Eight: Smooth Sleep Baby Sleep Approach, and focus on 'Step One: Establish the Best Foundation', to learn how to create a safe and soothing sleep haven for your little one.

3. Know the basics of baby sleep and what's to come during the first years of life so that you can have realistic expectations, and don't run into the most common mistakes parents make, such as creating habits that they later on need or want to break.

4. Forward thinking—consider breastfeeding as an option, as it's been proven better (in most cases) than formula (see my position on breastfeeding in the previous chapter). Condition yourself, and remember that once the baby comes, the best thing you can do with regards to sleep is to not create sleep habits or routines at the beginning that you will want to break down the road (i.e., rocking your baby to sleep, nursing until baby falls asleep, etc.). **Don't start anything that you are not willing to continue doing**.

I work with many expectant moms, who follow the Smooth Baby Sleep approach from day one; and most of them never have to do sleep training per se after the 4th month of life of their babies. Their children grow into healthy sleep habits from the beginning, so by the time they are physically ready to sleep through the night or settle on longer naps, they naturally do so.

ରୁ Thomas, 20 Months Old, and Rose, Newborn

One of my first clients, Amanda, hired me to help her with her then 20-month-old son, Thomas. Thomas didn't have great sleep habits, and he was keeping everybody up at night.

Amanda was pregnant with her second child, and she wanted help with Thomas before the second baby arrived. I worked with her and her family, and after about a week, Thomas was napping two hours every day, sleeping 11 hours straight at night, without crying-it-out, and he was a happy camper.

We also developed a plan to help her new baby develop healthy sleep habits from day one so that she didn't have to go thought the troubles she went through with Thomas. That plan included everything that I'm sharing with you in this book and more customized information.

Months later, Amanda contacted me again to let me know that her almost 5-month-old baby girl, Rose, was an amazing sleeper from the very beginning. She had followed the strategy we built together, and she never had to sleep train her daughter.

I wanted to share with you this story to show you that there are many things you can do from the time your baby arrives that have nothing to do with sleep training that will help your baby become a great sleeper.

Birth to 4 Weeks

Developmental Milestones

Your baby is still learning to be out of your womb. It might take her some time to learn how to breastfeed or bottle-feed. Most babies drop weight a couple of days after birth, but that weight is commonly recovered after 2 weeks. After that, most babies gain ½ to 1 ounce per day.

Parenting Tips

During your baby's first weeks of life, I'd advise you to take care of yourself, let yourself heal, and watch out for baby blues and postpartum depression. Enroll help and don't be afraid to be specific about what you and your baby need. Let your baby sleep and control visiting hours. Spend as much time as possible "learning" your baby and bonding with her.

I also encourage you to try **kangaroo care** and practice it as much as possible. Kangaroo care is a technique of holding the baby, skin to skin, that is usually practiced on newborns and premature babies. The baby is placed against the parent's chest, in an upright position, naked or with a diaper on; and with a blanket covering her back. The benefits of kangaroo care include improved bonding and closeness with your baby, increased breast milk supply, stabilized baby's heart rate, improved baby's breathing pattern, improved oxygen saturation levels, and increased weight gain, among others.

I similarly encourage you to learn **infant massage**, and practice it every day with your baby. You can do it any time of the day, although I've found it to be a great add-on to babies' bedtime routines. Baby massage helps soothe your baby, is a great way to bond with your baby, promotes the proper growth and healthy development of infants, stimulates your baby's nerves, increases her blood flow, strengthens her immune system, helps relieve colic, gas, and constipation, and much more.

Golden Pillars Specifics

✺ *Swaddle*

Swaddle your baby from the time she comes home from the hospital. The main purpose of swaddling your baby while she's a newborn is to make her feel secure, warm, and safe. After nine months inside your womb, your baby will feel disoriented in the outside world, and the swaddling will help her remember her previous environment and rest.

Swaddle your baby in a breathable blanket that is large enough to cover your baby and appropriate for the current weather conditions. As a rule of thumb, remember that babies should wear one more layer than adults. Do not overdress your baby, because overheating is a major risk factor for SIDS.

✺ *Pacifier*

If you are planning on breastfeeding your baby, wait until nursing is well established to introduce the pacifier.

162

Sleep Transitions & Healthy Sleep

The life of a newborn is spent alternating between two activities: sleeping and eating. When your baby is first born, the majority of his day is spent sleeping. Babies that are born premature can sleep even up to 20 hours a day!

Newborns don't really take naps at this stage because their periods of alertness are generally limited to the time when they are eating. Because newborns have small stomachs that can only hold tiny amounts of milk, they usually wake up every two and a half to four hours. It is therefore unrealistic, as well as unhealthy, to expect your newborn to sleep for eight or ten hours straight at night.

5 to 8 Weeks

Developmental Milestones

At this age, your baby can probably lift his head when lying on his tummy. He responds to sounds around him and turns to them. He follows objects across his field of vision. He starts vocalizing, and he gurgles and coos.

Sleep Transitions & Healthy Sleep

Have forward thinking; think about what your ideal situation in terms of your baby's sleep is, and move towards that scenario. Focus on creating positive and healthy sleep associations and on avoiding creating poor ones. If you know you don't want to co-sleep, don't bring your baby to your bed. If you know you don't want to nurse your baby to sleep, start breaking the latch before he falls asleep.

ᘓ Lola, 5 Weeks Old

Lola was the first child of Alice and George. Recently married, neither one of them really wanted to have children yet, but welcomed the addition when they realized they were expecting. When baby Alice was finally here, they were still in shock and denial about the baby. From the moment Lola was born, her mother described her as a very difficult baby. Alice pointed these as the main problems of her daughter:

"*She had trouble latching on and didn't want to breastfeed. She wouldn't like to stay in her crib by herself; she fussed a lot, and she cried for hours on end. She didn't sleep more than 30 minutes straight, and she was impossible to read.*"

Alice was a little desperate and didn't know what to do with Lola, even though many of the things Alice mentioned were typical of a baby that age. I sat down with them, trying to understand what a normal day looked like for Lola. Lola was 5 weeks old at that time.

Lola woke up, crying, at a different time every day, and Alice tried to breastfeed her. If it didn't work, she would hand her over to her night nurse for her to bottle feed her. This was the "modus operandi" for all her feedings. Every time Lola cried, Alice's first response was offering her the breast.

Alice and George had very large families. Alice is the youngest of 5 siblings, and George is the second of six. Therefore, their house was always filled with people visiting them and the baby. Additionally, they were determined to not change their lifestyle at all now that Lola was here. They continued having people over, staying up until very late at night, visiting with friends. They would even go out at night with Lola in the carrier.

In my opinion, Lola was overtired, sleep deprived, underfed and overwhelmed with all the action, movement and activity. Her day and night routines weren't determined by her internal clock or by her sleep and feeding needs; instead, her routine was determined by Alice and George's lifestyle and their friends and family schedule.

Alice and George were not happy when I told them that even though you don't stop being yourself when you become a parent, you do have to adjust your lifestyle to make sure you meet your child's needs. They were hesitant to follow my advice at first.

"When Diana told us that WE were the ones who had to make changes and that it wasn't about Lola but about US, we were irritated. We felt offended, and we were ready to part ways then and there. However, my mother, who had gifted us Diana's consultation, insisted that we give her plan a try. Reluctantly, we did."

I started with the basics, making them aware of Lola's sleep needs and prioritizing them, helping them learn her cues, establishing good sleep and feeding routines, and setting limits to the visits of their family and friends. Then, we moved on to structuring their day so that they all had time for themselves, and we incorporated bonding time and playing time in their schedule.

Lola welcomed the changes in her daily life. She stopped crying for hours on end, and she was happier, calmer, and better rested. Breastfeeding became much easier, and she was finally gaining weight consistently. Alice and George started feeling better as well, and they began enjoying their new role as parents.

"After the first week, I was more aware of her needs. I was able to read her cues better, and I loved spending time with her. One day, something shifted in my mind. I was breastfeeding Lola and our eyes met. I couldn't stop crying. I finally felt the bond most moms talk about. She was MY DAUGHTER, and I was HER MOM. Since that moment on, everything changed. We connected.

I would've never expected that my family would be transformed and that I would be transformed, after a sleep consultation, but it did. I still love to go out with my friends and have family over, and I still do it. However, now we do it in a way that makes the three of us happy. I am forever thankful to Diana for opening my eyes to what being a mom really is; and for giving me the tools to stop struggling as a mother and to find the joy and excitement in every day events."

Alice Payne
Philadelphia, PA

166

9 to 16 Weeks

Developmental Milestones

At this age, your little one recognizes the faces of his parents and scents. He is also able to hold his head steady, and he can lift his head and shoulders a little bit when lying on his tummy. He visually starts tracking objects and movement. Some babies start rolling at this age.

Golden Pillars Specifics

✑ *Swaddle*

After two to three months, many babies will start kicking and fighting the swaddle, while others are comfortable being "wrapped" until about 4 months. Whenever you see your baby fighting the swaddling while he's sleep or before falling asleep, it's your cue to stop swaddling.

Swaddling a baby becomes a safety hazard once your baby is able to roll over, which usually occurs between 2 and 5 months. Stop swaddling once your baby learns how to roll over. You don't want your baby to roll from his back to his tummy in the crib and end up swaddled face down. Therefore, once you notice that your baby can roll from his back to his tummy, stop swaddling.

ᕆ Crib

If you haven't done so yet, stop using a bassinet and transfer your child to a crib. This transition should occur before your baby can push up to her hands and knees or when she is physically too tight in the bassinet.

Sleep Transitions & Healthy Sleep

A more regular pattern of sleeping and eating usually begins to emerge around the second or third month of your baby's life. The longest sleep periods begin to stretch to between four and eight hours as healthy sleep habits begin to emerge. Naps begin during these months, and they usually settle into three-a-day schedule: morning, midday, and afternoon. Establishing healthy sleep habits is a primary goal during this time.

17 to 24 Weeks

Developmental Milestones

At this age, your baby smiles, laughs, squeals, and coos. She recognizes her own name and turns towards sounds and voices. She starts imitating sounds. She can bear weight on her legs, and she can roll both ways (back to tummy and tummy to back). She plays with her hands and her feet, and she sits with support.

Golden Pillars Specifics

You can introduce a lovey, safety blanket, or sleeping buddy at around 6-8 months, but not before, due to risks of suffocation. See the side box for further information on introducing a safe lovey.

Sleep Transitions & Healthy Sleep

Babies who are five to six months old have sleeping habits and needs that are markedly different from when they were first born. The great news for parents is that the longest sleep periods could last 10 to 12 hours at night.

Naptime is still a necessary part of your baby's schedule. Naps will decrease to around twice day, but they will increase in duration.

6 to 8 Months

Developmental Milestones

At nine months of age, your baby is more aware of her surroundings, and he interacts much more. She starts babbling and says 'mama' and 'dada'. She sits up without support and has more hand dexterity. She drags objects, crawls, and might begin to cruise while holding onto something.

Between six and eight months of age many babies develop separation anxiety. The best way to respond to your child's separation anxiety is by respecting and understanding her feelings and by reassuring her. Try to be with her as much as possible, and make her feel safe. If you have to leave, always say goodbye and make sure she is used to the person you leave her with.

At 6 months of age, most babies are ready to start solid foods and to start finger feeding. If your baby starts showing growing interest in what you are eating, can hold her head in a steady, upright position, and can sit without support, she might be ready to start supplementing her diet with some solid foods.

Start offering rice cereal or oatmeal diluted in breast milk or formula. Continue introducing pureed vegetables and fruits (avoid peaches). At around 9 months, you could also introduce some pureed meat. Make sure the transition is smooth—be patient, and do not force your child to eat anything. As suggested by nutritionist Ellyn Satter, the rule that I follow when it comes to feeding children is this: "Parents decide the what, the when, and the where, and children decide how much they eat."

Sleep Transitions & Healthy Sleep

By seven to nine months of age, most babies are able to sleep between ten and thirteen hours at night. Naptime remains consistent, and babies this age usually take two naps per day. As your baby approaches nine months of age, one nap might begin to shorten in duration as the other one lengthens.

Some babies go through a sleep regression at around 9 months of age, as they go through their first episodes of separation anxiety. If you haven't introduced a lovey yet, this is a good time to start. Wear the lovey under your clothes for a couple of days, and let your child see you with the lovey so that she associates it with you.

9 to 12 Months

Developmental Milestones

Most babies this age respond to simple verbal commands. They understand different tones, and they can differentiate between familiar and unfamiliar people and events. They might also imitate gestures, say "no," wave "bye, bye," and have a few more words. Most babies this age have better hand and eye coordination, have a better finger grasp, and can self-feed better. They can also start drinking from an open cup, and by the time they turn 12 months, they are ready to drop the bottles and drink all their liquids from a sippy cup or straw cup.

Most also can sit without assistance, are proficient creepers or crawlers, can pull themselves to standing position, can cruise along furniture or holding on to your hand, and most start walking.

Babies this age are much more aware of their surroundings, and they are able to express their likes and dislikes. You might even notice that one of their favorite words is "no."

Twelve months is another critical age when it comes to "separation anxiety." Remember that separation anxiety is a normal part of development. As mentioned above, generally the way babies handle separation is a direct reflection of how their parents handle it. Make sure you handle it the best you can, without feeding into the drama. Practice separation by leaving her with familiar people in familiar places. Always say, "Goodbye" when you leave, and "I'm back. Mommy always comes back," when you come back. Reassure your child as much as you can, and know that as unbearable as this phase can be at times, it's just a phase. It too shall pass. Believe me, when it does, you will miss those hugs and focused attention.

Sleep Transitions & Healthy Sleep

Babies who are nine to twelve months old continue to enjoy an extended period of nighttime sleep that is between ten and twelve hours. Naptimes are still an important part of your baby's day.

At this age, some babies will still need two naps per day, but one nap will likely be of shorter duration than the other. It is also possible that your baby will have given up one of his naps and be down to just one nap a day. If your baby has dropped down to just one nap, this naptime will be of longer duration than previous naps.

13 to 18 Months

Developmental Milestones

Most babies this age adequately use several words, love pretend games, "read" books, like riding toys, scribble with a crayon, and point to body parts. They can run, walk backwards, and start jumping in place.

They can also eat with their fingers, start using a fork and a spoon, and can also start drinking from an open cup. By the time they turn 12 months, they are ready to drop the bottles, and drink all their liquids from a sippy cup or straw cup. Also at 12 months, most babies can be transitioned to whole milk.

This is the age when temper tantrums begin, because their brains and minds go beyond what their physical abilities can do. They get frustrated because they can't do all the things they think they can do. They also have a newfound sense of independence and willfulness, which makes them use the word "no" more often and challenge your decisions. Allow them to make decisions whenever possible.

"Separation anxiety" peaks at 18 months. Remember that separation anxiety is a normal part of development. As mentioned above, generally, the way babies handle separation is a direct reflection of how their parents handle it. Make sure you handle it the best you can, without feeding into the drama. Practice separation by leaving her with familiar people in familiar places. Always say, "Goodbye" when you leave, and "I'm back. Mommy always comes back," when you come back. Reassure your child as much as you can, and know that as unbearable as this phase can be at times, it's just a phase. It too shall pass. Believe me, when it does, you will miss those hugs and focused attention.

Sleep Transitions & Healthy Sleep

Nighttime sleep patterns remain consistent after the first year of life, leveling off at between ten to twelve hours per night. Most toddlers drop their morning nap somewhere between 15 to 18 months of age.

ଔ Nate, 14 Months Old (Preemie, Born at 27 Weeks Gestation)

"By the time our son Nate was 14 months old, his sleep problems had become intolerable. Nate's sleep issues included his inability to fall asleep on his own, his reluctance to go in his crib unless fully asleep, and his inconsistent nap routine.

Bedtime was Nate's biggest challenge. Once he was in his crib, Nate would have constant night wakings. He would usually wake up crying 3 to 4 times a night. My husband and I would take turns holding him and rocking him back to sleep, sometimes for an hour. We would also end up feeding him during these wakings in hopes of settling him down.

By the time 5am would come, we would just give up, and Nate was awake for the day. These night wakings, along with the night feedings were ruining Nate's daytime schedule. His naps and meals were affected, and he was cranky from lack of sleep. Nate's naptimes were just as difficult as he needed to be held for the duration of the entire nap.

My husband and I were exhausted and frustrated. I did lots of research and read many books to try and find some solutions. However, I kept finding conflicting information, and I did not know what method would work best for us. That is where Diana came in. Diana was sympathetic and understanding, and she spent a long time with us discussing Nate's schedule. She tailored a detailed sleep plan and schedule to meet Nate's particular needs.

After meeting with Diana, my husband and I finally had a plan. We were prepared for a tough road ahead. On the first night, Nate still had 3 night wakings, but he was actually able to fall right back asleep without our help. By the second night, he was sleeping through the night, completely uninterrupted! We continued to be consistent, and within a few days, Nate was not only sleeping in his crib at night but also during nap times as well. We have been following the plan ever since, and currently, Nate sleeps about 11 and a half hours at night and takes 2 naps that are between an hour to an hour and a half long.

I am so happy that I contacted Diana. A good night's sleep has not only helped Nate become a happier, well rested boy, but it has improved our whole family's life!"

Michal K.
New York, NY. USA

19 Months to 2 Years

Developmental Milestones

Most children this age master the use of up to 100 words, and they start combining them into two to three word sentences. In fact, half of their speech is commonly understandable. They love pretend play. They can follow directions, but they also love to exercise their newfound higher degree of independence. They can use a spoon and fork, and they can drink from an open cup—therefore, self-feeding.

Sleep Training Toddlers

We often come across parents of toddlers who wonder whether their children are already too old to be sleep-trained. The answer is "no!" It is never too late to teach your children healthy sleep habits. Truth be told, the older the child, the more challenging the process is going to be. However, it is certainly possible.

Here are some things you need to take into consideration when sleep training an older toddler:

- They need to sleep.
- They learn from us. Children model our behavior, so make sure you are a good example in the sleep arena too.
- They are smart. They will try everything under the sun to get your attention and get their way.

- They love their independence, making decisions, and being involved in what's going on in their lives.

What method should you follow? I do not believe "cry-it-out" is the best method for sleep training babies; although, we acknowledge that it might work with some babies*. When it comes to toddlers, it just doesn't work! You need to create a plan that involves your child and that is adapted to your child's personality; otherwise, it won't work. These are some things to keep in mind when building your plan:

- You are trying to break a habit that you helped create.
- They understand, so get them on board! Get them excited about sleep. Make feel "adult-like."
- Consistency and patience are key.
- Avoid fights and stay calm.
- Do not negotiate at bedtime.
- Make it fun, praise them, and reward them every morning for the first weeks.
- Make sure the room is childproof.

❧ *Visual Bedtime Routine:* **Bedtime Routine Mural**

Once you've decided on the best schedule for your child, get him involved in choosing the steps she wants to add to the bedtime routine. Do not offer her options you are not comfortable with; for example, watching TV before bedtime or mom lying on the bed with her shouldn't be an option.

Once you both have come up with a routine, create a mural with pictures of the different steps of her bedtime routine and go with her over it, every day. Before you start implementing the new routine, practice every step and take a picture. Once you have all the pictures, stick them in order on a large piece of paper, with the help of your child. You can also add numbers to each part of the routine.

Get your child as involved as possible in the process of making the picture routine mural. For example, your child can help you stick the pictures on the paper. Make sure you put a time for each of the steps in the bedtime routine, and create a beginning and end time for the whole routine.

When the mural is done, hang it close to the bathroom or bedroom so that she can see it when she starts the bedtime routine. During the first days, walk her through the pictures during the day, and tell her what the steps are going to be at night. At night, let her lead the process of getting to bed. Ask her, "*What do we have to do next?*" She can then go to the mural and tell you what comes next. Every morning, praise her for following the routine the night before.

⁓ *Transition from Crib to Toddler Bed*

Making the transition to a "big boys/girls bed" can be difficult, and many parents stress about this process. My advice is to keep your toddler in a crib for as long as possible; this means waiting until your toddler is around 3 years old. Therefore, I don't recommend you go through this process at this age. However, if you have already decided you are going to do it, please go to the next section (2 to 3 Years) and go over my suggestions for a peaceful and gentle transition.

2 to 3 Years

Developmental Milestones

At this age, most children walk easily, run well, jump with both feet, and balance on one foot. Most can also wash their hands and face, draw vertical lines, horizontal lines, and circles, open and close doors, put on and take off some clothes; learn songs; and understand descriptions and adjectives. They use long sentences, and start asking "why?"

Most kids this age go through potty training, and they start preschool. Temper tantrums and limit-testing are common at this age.

Sleep Training Toddlers

We often come across parents of toddlers who wonder whether their children are already too old to be sleep-trained. The answer is "no!" It is never too late to teach your children healthy sleep habits. Truth be told, the older the child, the more challenging the process is going to be. However, it is certainly possible.

Here are some things you need to take into consideration when sleep training an older toddler:

♦ They need to sleep.
♦ They learn from us. Children model our behavior; so make sure you are a good example in the sleep arena too.

- They are smart. They will try everything under the sun to get your attention and get their way.
- They love their independence, making decisions, and being involved in what's going on in their lives.

What method should you follow? I do not believe "cry-it-out" is the best method for sleep training babies; although, we acknowledge that it might work with some babies*. When it comes to toddlers, it just doesn't work! You need to create a plan that involves your child and that is adapted to your child's personality; otherwise, it won't work. These are some things to keep in mind when building your plan:

- You are trying to break a habit that you helped create.
- They understand, so get them on board! Get them excited about sleep. Make feel "adult-like."
- Consistency and patience are key.
- Avoid fights and stay calm.
- Do not negotiate at bedtime.
- Make it fun, praise them, and reward them every morning for the first weeks.
- Make sure the room is childproof.

๑ *Visual Bedtime Routine:* **Bedtime Routine Mural**

Once you've decided on the best schedule for your child, get him involved in choosing the steps she wants to add to the bedtime routine. Do not offer her options you are not comfortable with; for example, watching TV before bedtime or mom lying on the bed with her shouldn't be an option.

Once you both have come up with a routine, create a mural with pictures of the different steps of her bedtime routine and go with her over it, every day. Before you start implementing the new routine, practice every step and take a picture. Once you have all the pictures, stick them in order on a large piece of paper, with the help of your child. You can also add numbers to each part of the routine.

Get your child as involved as possible in the process of making the picture routine mural. For example, your child can help you stick the pictures to the paper. Make sure you put a time for each of the steps in the bedtime routine, and create a beginning and end time for the whole routine.

When the mural is done, hang it close to the bathroom or bedroom so that she can see it when she starts the bedtime routine. During the first days, walk her through the pictures during the day, and tell her what the steps are going to be at night. At night, let her lead the process of getting to bed. Ask her, "What do we have to do next?" She can then go to the mural and tell you what comes next. Every morning, praise her for following the routine the night before.

❧ Transition from Crib to Toddler Bed

When should you do it?

Making the transition to a "big boys/girls bed" can be difficult, and many parents stress about this process. Our advice is to keep your toddler in a crib for as long as possible; this means waiting until your toddler is around 3 years old.

There's no one-size-fits-all recommendation to tell parents when a child is ready to make the move from a crib to a bed. Every child is different, and you know yours better than anyone. Wait to make the transition once you feel she's ready, and she'll be able to do it without major complications. Some signs that she's ready are the following:

- She's been trying to climb out of her crib consistently at night and naps (crib tents and mattress on the lowest position didn't work).
- She understands directions and boundaries.
- She shows interest in the beds of other friends or siblings.

When shouldn't you do it?

When there's another major change or event going on (i.e., new sibling, new house, potty training, new daycare, new caregiver, etc.).

How's that process going to affect her sleep habits?

Some toddlers will enjoy their newfound freedom and jump out of the bed and roam around; some will feel afraid of being taken out of the safety of their familiar crib; and some will transition easily to their new beds, sleeping there from day one.

Sleep training and sleep adjustments are different for every one of us. Keep in mind that your child will eventually sleep in her bed. Make a plan of how the transition is going to go and stick to it.

How do you do it?

We advise you to break it down in different phases:

1. Preparation:

During the **preparation** you should talk to your child about moving to a "big bed" and how great that is. You should make it sound like a big accomplishments to her. Tell other family members and friends what a big girl she is and that you trust her so much that you're going to give her a "big girl bed." Your goal is trying to get her to feel proud about the transition. Create anticipation. You can mention older friends, siblings, or friends who sleep in a bed. Remind your child how big and grown up she is now, and remind her of other milestones that she has reached (i.e., potty training, giving up a pacifier, drinking by herself, brushing her teeth, dressing herself, etc.)

If possible, try to involve your child in the process. Let her pick the bed and the sheets, and let her choose between two different locations where the bed should go in the room. Decide what to do with her crib; decide how she wants to say "goodbye" to her crib; take pictures of her in the crib, etc.

Make sure her bedroom is "safe" before making the transition. As she will be mobile, you have to make sure that she won't be able to harm herself if she decides to move around at night or during naps.

Pick a date in which you will make the transition, and make a fun countdown with your child. She could cross off the days on the calendar, write the number of days left on a board, etc.

2. Mixing It Up:

During this phase, you should let her familiarize with her new surroundings without making the transition. This means, letting her use the new sheets and pillow while she's still sleeping in the crib. Remember to celebrate and to take pictures of every step towards the transition.

3. Transition:

There are many different approaches for how to do the transition. However, I believe that the most effective for most kids is the "cold turkey" approach. On the day you and your child decide the transition will take place, talk about it from the moment your child awakes in the morning. Set up the new bed (or take down the side from the convertible bed), have her help you make the bed, arrange the pillows, etc.... If you are removing the old crib, you can throw it a "goodbye" party. Start the transition at nap time that first day, and celebrate after the nap is over—even if she fought it a little bit before falling asleep. Remember, have your same routines in place!

Remember:

- If you think your child is ready, and you decide to make the transition, stick to that decision (no going back!).
- Take the crib away once the transition is done (out of sight means out of mind).
- Celebrate your child's accomplishment in the morning.
- Make a big deal out of it.
- Keep your bedtime routine in place. You can also incorporate the bed into the routine (i.e., reading time now is on the bed).
- Do not put "bad associations" in your child's head. She might not think that it's going to be scary, so don't suggest it by saying things like, "Don't worry, you don't have to be scared." She might not even think of coming out of bed, so don't tell her, "You can't come out of the bed."

- If your child has a convertible crib, the transition should be easier, since she will still be in her familiar "crib."
- If your child comes out of the bed, bring her back, calmly but firmly.

Remember that moving to a "big bed" is one of the many milestones your child will accomplish in the first years of life. Our experience tells us that the attitude the parents have towards the transition determines how easy or hard the process will be. So, try to be relaxed about it; feel proud of your child; know you both can do it; and do it!

Special Note for Co-Sleeping Families

If your child is co-sleeping, there's not really an age at which the transition to a crib or toddler bed is necessary or advisable. There are three situations in which making the transition is advisable:

1. The child, the parents, or all are having poor quality sleep. They are not comfortable. They have constant night awakenings. They don't have a good night's sleep, and they resent their sleeping situation.
2. The child shows interest in having his own bed.
3. The parents do not feel comfortable with the sleeping situation anymore; they need more intimacy; there's another baby that needs co-sleeping, etc.

If you've been sharing your bed with your child, and you think now it's the right time to make the transition, there are many ways to go about this transition. After working with many families in this situation, out of all the approaches out there, I've found one to be easier on both parents and children; therefore, that one would be my recommendation. This approach breaks down the

186

transition into different phases, and it assumes that you establish a new bedtime routine, as mentioned before. The first phase's goal would be to get your child to sleep in his own room. The way to do it is by bringing a mattress to your child's bedroom and putting it by his toddler bed. Therefore, at the beginning, your child will be within touching distance from you, at the same level, but on a different mattress. In fact, the first couple of days, he won't even be in his bed, he'll be lying down with you on the mattress. As he feels more and more comfortable sleeping like that, you can start phase two.

Phase two's goal is to have your child sleeping in his own bed, while you're still sleeping in his bedroom. You can still hold her hand and be within touching distance. However, you're on different mattresses and he eventually sleeps consistently on his bed. Then you would start moving your mattress further and further away from your child's bed, until you are by the door, and eventually in your own bedroom. The goal is to move it a little bit each day, at a pace that your child is comfortable with. Some families start on phase one without the mattress by the child's bed, and placing a chair or sofa there instead. This is the sleep method described previously, called the "Side-by-Side" Approach.

Scheduling Guidelines

As children begin to near the age of three, many of them begin to resist naptime. Protect their afternoon naps for as long as you can, but realize that most children drop their final nap by age three.

3 to 5 Years

Sleep Transitions & Healthy Sleep

Preschoolers usually transition from their cribs to a toddler bed at around three years of age if they have not already done so. During this period, it is important to be patient with your child and realize that some sleep retraining may be necessary. Reinforcing a clear bedtime routine is also imperative during this time. All children thrive on routines, but preschoolers in particular find them very reassuring.

Help your child learn to recognize the difference in the way she feels, in the way she concentrates, in the way she remembers things, in the way she is able to enjoy herself, and in the way she feels after losing sleep or not getting a healthy sleep. The ability to self-reflect and understand one's own body responses is a precious tool for everyone, and it is never too early to practice it.

BUILD YOUR CHILD'S CUSTOMIZED SMOOTH SLEEP PLAN

"Good plans shape good decisions. That's why good planning helps to make elusive dreams come true."

- LESTER ROBERT BITTEL

Have you ever heard the old proverb, "If you fail to plan, you plan to fail?" This concept is true in life, and it is true for training your baby to sleep. The final and most important strategy that I want you to consider before we delve into the Smooth Baby Sleep method is to have a written plan before the first night of sleep training!

If it seems overwhelming to contemplate writing your decisions down NOW, imagine having to make important choices about your plan in the middle of the night. It is much more productive to craft a clear plan and agree on responsibilities when all caregivers are clear-headed and can reach an agreement. Arguments or intense discussions about whose turn it is to feed the baby are exceptionally counterproductive at three in the morning.

Please take the time to download and complete the Smooth Baby Sleep worksheets, templates, and guidelines, by visiting our website www.SmoothBabySleepBook.com. Once there, you will need to introduce the code SBSBOOK. You can also find a template in the Appendix of this book.

Remember Your Goals & Expectations

Start describing your current situation, challenges, and the summary of key findings from your child's daily logs with regards to her sleep health. Continue describing your goals and what your ideal situation is. For some, the desired situation might be the baby sleeping 12 hours at night in his own room. For others, it might be to continue co-sleeping but to reduce the night waking. For others, it might be having the baby sleep in his older brother's bedroom without waking up. For others, it might be the baby waking up later in the morning. Write down that end goal, being as specific as possible. As the sleep training days go by, revisit this section of the plan to see your progress.

Enlist Everyone and Divide Responsibilities

During the sleep training process, assign responsibilities. You can decide one parent does the first night and the other the second one, or you can decide one does the first half of the night and the other one the second half. Whatever responsibilities breakdown works for you is fine. Just make sure that you go over it and write it down. You also need to decide whether you need coaching, assistance, some sort of support system, etc. This can be in the form of a friend, family member, or a sleep consultant.

If your child's unhealthy sleep associations are with mom, then it's advisable for dad or grandma (somebody other than mom) to take care of the first two-three nights of sleep training, especially with babies who breastfeed. This is just a recommendation. I've worked with many single parents, who don't have anyone to help them with the sleep coaching program. They are just as successful, and their children become independent sleepers as well.

Put It In Writing

This is baby Abigail's customized Smooth Baby Sleep Plan:

Current Situation
Abigail can't fall asleep on her own, doesn't have consistent naps, and wakes up frequently during naps and an average of 5 times during the night. She cries and gets fussy quite often during the day.
Abigail is sleep deprived. She is sleeping an average of 2 to 3 hours less than she should during the day and 1 to 3 less than she should during the night.

Desired Situation: Right Expectations & Goals
Abigail isn't sleep deprived. She sleeps 10 to 12 hours during the night and 4 to 6 hours during the day, divided into two naps.
Abigail happily falls asleep by herself every night without crying or parental assistance. She doesn't wake up in the middle of the night, and if she does, she puts herself back to sleep without fussing and without our help. She happily takes two restorative, long naps per day, without complaining or crying.
She is happy, well rested, active, and alert during the day. She feels loved, attached, safe, and secure, and the bond between her and her parents is intact.

Appropriate Attitude & Mindset

1. Be calm, patient, and nurturing.
2. Be open-minded and willing.
3. Be consistent.
4. Make sleep a priority.
5. Don't expect miracles.

Calming, Bonding, and Safe Sleep Rituals

1. Continue putting her back to sleep.
2. Continue offering her the pacifier, but teach her to grab it.
3. Get rid of the mobile and the CD to get her to sleep.
4. Bedtime routine (after dinner – solid foods):
    a. Give her a relaxing bath.
    b. Go to the nursery with dimmed lights.
    c. Give her a soothing massage.
    d. Put her pajamas and diaper on.
    e. Give her the bottle while you read her a book.
    f. Burp her and give her the pacifier and her lovey.
    g. Turn off the lights.
    h. Rock her and sing to her 2 bedtime songs ("Twinkle, Twinkle, Little Star" and "Lullaby").
    i. Put her down to sleep when she's drowsy but still awake.
5. Nap time routine:
    a. Go to the nursery with dimmed lights.
    b. Change her diaper and put her sleep sack on.
    c. Read her a book.
    d. Turn off the lights.
    e. Rock her and sing to her 2 bedtime songs ("Twinkle, Twinkle, Little Star" and "Lullaby").
    f. Put her down to sleep, drowsy but still awake.

Safe and Soothing Sleep Haven

1. Darken the room more during sleep time.
2. Install a thermometer and make sure it's not too hot or cold.
3. Place the monitor a little bit further away.

Everyone on Board

List all the people who currently take care of Abigail on occasions and during her naps and/or bedtime.

1. Caregivers: Mom, Dad, Grandma Sara, Nana, Grandpa Tom, Ally, Auntie Susan, Danielle, Maria, and Uncle Tim
2. Pediatrician: Dr. Robin

Starting Date

Friday, October 9th

Schedule

Time	Day (Hours)
6:00am	Waking Time
6:00am	Bottle
6:30am	Solids
	Active Play
8 am – 9am	Morning Nap
	Active Play
10:30am	Bottle
11am	Solids
11:30am – 1:30pm	Mid-day Nap
1:30pm	Bottle
	Play
4:30pm	Solids
5:00pm	Bath + Massage + Pajamas
5:30pm	Bottle
6:00pm	Bedtime
6pm-6am	Sleep

Sleep Coaching Method:
Regular Comfort & Reassurance

1. Ten to twenty minutes before nap time or bedtime, bring baby to the nursery.

2. Before you start the soothing sleep routine, let her know that it is time to sleep now, that after your routine she will stay there in her crib, and that you will leave, but you will stay nearby if she needs you.

3. Follow your daily sleep routine. This can mean changing her diaper, putting comfy pajamas on, singing a lullaby, hugging, rocking for a little bit, reading a book... whatever you have decided that your bedtime routine would be.

4. Put her in the crib, saying comforting words ("I love you, time to sleep now..."). You can pat her back for half a minute to a minute.

5. If she starts crying, wait for (*first check-in*) minutes to go in back again and reassure her. You can pat her back and "shh" her (but do not pick her up) for 30 to 60 seconds. This time, you can say again, "Night, night. It's time to sleep." Your goal is not to get her to sleep. Your goal is to let her know that you are there if she really needs you, but it's time to sleep.

6. If she starts crying once you leave the room, wait (*second check-in*) minutes outside.

7. If after that time she is still crying, go inside and repeat Step 4, without talking this time. If she's not crying or if you feel she's calming down on her own, don't go inside. For example, if she's talking or making noises, fussing but not crying, don't go in. This might cause her to get worked up again.

8. If she starts crying again once you leave the room, wait (*third check-in*) minutes outside.

9. If after that time she is still crying, go inside and repeat Step 4, without talking this time. If she's not crying or if you feel she's calming down on her own, don't go inside. For example, if

she's talking or making noises, fussing but not crying, don't go in. This might cause her to get worked up again.

10. If she starts crying again once you leave the room, repeat Steps 8 and 9, until your baby is either calmed or sleeping.

Breakdown of Responsibilities

	Morning Nap	Mid-day Nap	Bedtime	Night Wakings
Day 1	X	X	Dad	Dad
Day 2	Mom	Mom	Dad	Dad
Day 3	Mom	Mom	Dad	Dad
Day 4	Nana	Nana	Mom	Mom
Day 5	Nana	Nana	Mom	Mom
Day 6	Mom	Mom	Mom	Mom
Day 7	Mom	Mom	Dad	Dad
Day 8	Auntie Susan	Auntie Susan	Dad	Dad
Day 9	Dad	Dad	Mom	Mom
Day 10	Mom	Mom	Dad	Dad
Day 11	Nana	Mom	Mom	Mom
Day 12	Mom	Nana	Mom	Mom
Day 13	Mom	Nana	Mom	Mom
Day 14	Mom	Mom	Dad	Dad
Day 15	Auntie Susan	Auntie Susan	Dad	Dad

IMPLEMENTATION

Step Six

MAKE IT HAPPEN & FOLLOW THROUGH

"Our children are counting on us to provide two things: consistency and structure. Children need parents who say what they mean, mean what they say, and do what they say they are going to do."

- BARBARA COLOROSO

Consistency

I feel the need to remind you again that your consistency is essential for your child's sleep success. **Consistency, calmness, patience, trust, and reassurances are essential in helping your child become an independent sleeper.** You are doing what's best for your child; stay calm and believe he can become a great sleeper.

Remember that your goal is **not** to get your child to sleep. Your goal is to create the right environment, follow the right routines, and reassure her, so she falls asleep on her own. The task of falling asleep is on her, not on you.

Once you decide on a method, stick to it for at least 7 days. Follow it during the day and during the whole night. Follow the same steps when she wakes up in the middle of a nap or during the night until waking time. Do not respond differently to your child at 5am than you would at 2am. If you do, you will be sending her a confusing message, which might increase the crying.

For the first days of sleep training, I recommend you to not do sleep training. I know this might sound contradictory, but as I mentioned before, for the first days, I want you to focus on implementing your child's perfect schedule in a consistent way. **Once you've been following the schedule for 3-5 days, you can pick a date to start with sleep training and stick to it.** I usually recommend parents to start on a Friday, as the first two-three days of sleep training are the hardest ones. You might need the free time to take a rest during the day. Start sleep training at dinnertime on the first day and continue following the schedule from then on. Do not begin sleep training with a nap; always start at bedtime.

During the first two weeks of sleep training, keep the schedule as consistent as possible, and keep your child's sleep environment and conditions as consistent as possible. Avoid travel, sleepovers, and naps on the go during those first two weeks.

Respond to Your Child's Basic Needs

As I mentioned before, I do believe that there's always a reason behind a child's cry. That doesn't mean that we have to respond to all the cries in the same way, but we do need to acknowledge the fact that when our baby cries, it is for a reason. You have to be particularly aware of this idea when you start sleep training. Make sure your baby's basic needs are covered before you put him to sleep. Guarantee that she is not crying out of hunger, out of discomfort, or out of pain. If your baby is hungry, you should always feed her. If she needs a diaper change, you should change her. Many sleep consultants will tell you to leave her sleep with her soiled or wet diaper. I respectfully disagree with this idea. I advise parents to change their child's diapers if that's making her uncomfortable. Even if your baby is not uncomfortable, I would encourage you to change a soiled diaper if you smell it.

Make the diaper change boring, gentle, with as little light as possible, and as fast as possible. Try not to overextend this moment and take advantage of it to give extra cuddling, to talk or sing to your baby, or to engage with your baby. It should be a seamless transition: out of the crib, diaper change, and back in the crib.

If you child vomits during the sleep training process, because of the crying, because she got anxious, or because she knows that will bring you back inside the room, you should change her and change everything that is dirty. Again, many sleep consultants will disagree with me, and they will tell you to let her stay uncomfortable and sit in her own vomit. I don't see the point in doing that. If you see your child trying to do it on purpose, say "no" and go on with the sleep plan you've decided on.

If she ends up vomiting, do the same thing I mentioned before about the diaper change. Change everything that is dirty, do it gently and without anger, do not engage in conversations, and do not share comments about how that shouldn't be done. Clean everything up, change your child, put her back in the crib, and go on with the process.

Now, this is not as common as you might think. Many parents are concerned that their child is going to throw up if they try to sleep train her, but it's really not that common. This recommendation obviously doesn't apply when your child is sick and vomiting for a reason, such as when she has a stomach virus. In that case, you should not only change your child and clean up the surroundings, but you should also do everything possible to comfort your baby and make her feel better.

Results & Adjustments

"I am not discouraged because every wrong attempt discarded is another step forward."
- THOMAS EDISON

Tracking is not only important before you start sleep training your child, but it's also important during the first weeks of the sleep training process. Your goal is to continue keeping a daily log for the first three weeks of sleep training or until your baby becomes an independent sleeper. This information is instrumental for you during sleep training. It will allow you to identify what is working and what's not, and it will inspire you and encourage you to continue as you see the progress your child has made.

After the first four to six of days of sleep training and every three to four days thereafter, go back to your plan, and review your child's initial situation. This is important because as things get better, most people tend to forget how bad things were and where they started. Ask yourself, *"Has there been any progress or improvement?"*

If your answer is, "Yes, my child has reached our ideal situation in terms of sleep," congratulations! From now on, continue following your routines and schedules, paying attention to your child and his development, reinforcing your child's new healthy sleep habits.

If your answer is, "Yes, but the situation is not perfect yet" or "No, there's been no improvement," ask yourself the following questions to determine what you can improve and whether something needs to be changed:

- Have I been consistently implementing my child's Smooth Baby Sleep Plan for at least five to seven days?
- Have I implemented and followed the Smooth Baby Sleep Golden Pillars?
- Have I been committed to making a change?
- Have I been patient, loving, and caring during the process?
- Has everyone been on the same page?
- Is the schedule the right one for my baby?
- Is the chosen sleep training method the most appropriate for my family and for my baby?
- Is my child healthy (are there no medical issues interfering with my baby's sleep)?

If your response to any of those questions is "*No*," think about what you need to change and focus on. Then, start over. After another four to six days, review your results again. If, at some point, you get frustrated because nothing is working, take a break and rethink your whole plan after a couple of weeks.

Finally, if nothing seems to be working, seek help if you need it. Parents are not used to asking for advice or help, even when they are drowning, exhausted, and at their wits' end. If you feel overwhelmed or if you feel like nothing is working, seek help! Join support groups, read books, meet other parents, hire a sitter, ask a family member or friend to come help, hire a parenting coach or sleep consultant, talk to your pediatrician... or whatever you need to do to feel that you're in control again and that you are being the parent that you've always wanted to be, raising a happy, healthy, well-adjusted child.

Accountability

> *"There can be no true response without responsibility; there can be no responsibility without response."*
> - ARTHUR VOGEL

Accountability is always a big part of any plan you want to follow. That's why I make sure I email or talk to my elite, private clients every day as they implement their child's sleep training plan. I do this not only because I can get information as to how the plan is working, but also, because it helps them be accountable and follow through with what they've said they were going to do to improve their child's sleep habits. Additionally, it gives them encouragement and strength to stay the course.

Therefore, I would encourage you to find someone you can touch base with every morning and talk about how sleep training went. It could be a friend who is also sleep training her child. It could be one of the moms in your support group. It could be one of your colleagues at work. It could be your mom. It could be your spouse. Or, you could even share your progress with us on Facebook, at http://www.Facebook.com/SmoothParenting. Make sure that the person you choose as your "accountability buddy" understands and supports what you are doing, and that they are not there to judge what you've decided to do but to help you do it.

When to Start Sleep Training

You can start helping your baby develop healthy sleep habits from day one. During the early months of your baby's life, she sleeps pretty much all the time. There is actually very little that can be done to "force" a new baby to sleep when she wants to be awake, and conversely, there is very little that can be done to wake a baby up when she wants to be asleep.

However, there are many things you can do during the first months of life to help her learn to self-soothe and develop positive sleep associations that might actually prevent you from ever having to follow a tears-sleep training method at all. Doesn't that sound wonderful? I went over how to do this step by step, and I covered what you should and shouldn't do at every age, in Chapter Eight/ Step 4: Apply Age by Age Considerations.

When Not to Start Sleep Training

You shouldn't try to change or improve your child's sleep habits during a period of major change, as achieving success will be difficult. If your family is undergoing a major stressor like divorce, unemployment, potty training, vacation, the birth of a new sibling, or moving to a new home, put off formal sleep training until you are able to devote the majority of your attention to the process.

Please do not start sleep training if your child is sick or running a fever. There are certain illnesses and conditions that can interfere with your child's sleep quality, like the following: nasal congestion, teething, ear infections, colic, GERD, yeast or urinary tract infections, sleep apnea, night terrors, milk allergies, and more.

For a detailed list of conditions that affect sleep and what steps can be taken to minimize their impact, please review Chapter 8, which discusses special considerations.

How Long Sleep Training Takes

You need at least two to three weeks of uninterrupted, consistent effort to guarantee that your child settles on healthy sleep habits, especially when he has already developed negative sleep associations. By this I mean, no travel, no weekends away, no dinner at a friend's house, no grandparents visiting, no moving— nothing that departs from your normal routine should be happening during your first two to three weeks of sleep training.

This doesn't mean that it is going to take you two to three weeks to improve the situation. In fact, it tends to take just a few days, However, you need to make sure that you block your calendar and that you are consistent for those two to three weeks straight to avoid setbacks and old habits coming back.

You can see a table below with the averages of the families I personally work with to give you an indication. Among the families that I've worked with, sleep training has taken an average of 5 to 7 days. However, it can take more or less time for your child. The method that you decide to follow (I'll go over the main methods I use and recommend), and your child's age will directly impact the length of the process.

As a general rule, the more gentle, no-tears methods tend to take much longer than other methods. Additionally, the older the child is, the longer it usually takes. The following are the average times among the families we've worked with (including all methods):

Child's Age	Average Days of Sleep Training
4-8 months old	3 days
8-12 months old	6 days
12-30 months old	10 days
31 months old and up	15 days

Figure 21: Smooth Baby Sleep – Average Sleep Training Time

When you are ready to start, you've gone through this book, and have your customized plan ready, pick a start date and stick to it. My favorite days to start are Fridays, as the first days are usually the hardest. This way, you have the weekend to take turns sleeping and to get some rest before going back to work on Monday. Having said that, if you are already barely sleeping and if you are dragging yourself to work every morning on just a few hours of sleep after being up with your baby all night; you can certainly start any day! Just pick a day and stick to it.

Remember that changing a habit takes time, and things might get worse before they get better. **Keep in mind that as long as you are consistent and you follow your child's cues and your instincts, the smooth baby sleep approach will work for your family. By giving your child the ability to develop healthy sleep habits and a good quality sleep, you are doing what is best for her. .**

PART IV:

COMMON AND SPECIAL CIRCUMSTANCES

Chapter Nine

COMMON SLEEP CHALLENGES

"You can't expect to meet the challenges of today with yesterday's tools and expect to be in business tomorrow."

- UNKOWN AUTHOR

Illnesses and Pains

In this section, I will go over common illnesses and pains that your child might have and might interfere with her sleep. I will also share with you the best way to address sleep training (if at all possible) as your baby goes through them.

As a general rule, I would not advise you to start sleep training while your baby is sick or in pain. I would also encourage you to do whatever you need to do to make your child feel better while he is sick. That might mean holding upright a baby who is suffering from severe gastrointestinal reflux, for twenty minutes after you feed him, even though that might mean that he will fall asleep on you. Once your baby starts feeling better and you see signs of improvement, start cutting back on your assistance to help him sleep. You can go back to your healthy sleep habits or start sleep training once he is healthy.

What should you do if you have all the right customized routines, schedules, and positive sleep associations in place, and you are being consistent in your sleep training; yet your baby still has problems falling asleep, wakes up frequently, and doesn't rest well at night? I would encourage you to go through this list of illnesses and check with your doctor. My guess would be that there's an underlying medical condition interfering with your child's sleep.

Nasal Congestion

Nasal breathing is essential for infants; they need to breathe through their noses while they are feeding and while they are sucking on their pacifiers to soothe themselves. Severe nasal congestion may interfere with sleep. I wouldn't advise you to start sleep training if your child is congested.

Ear Infections

Ear infections cause mild to severe pain, as fluid builds up in the area behind your baby's eardrum and then becomes infected, which may disrupt your child's sleep.

A change in your child's mood (she is more fussy, she cries more often, she is more clingy, etc.), a high fever, pulling and grabbing her ears, mild or severe diarrhea, reduced appetite, a yellow or white fluid draining from her ear, and/or a foul odor coming from the ear are common signs of ear infections.

If you notice any of these signs in your baby, take her to the pediatrician for a sick baby visit. He will be able to diagnose her and give you something to ease her pain. Pacifier use may increase the risk of middle ear infections in babies and young children.

Colic

More and more often, I hear parents say that they have colicky babies, simply because their baby is crying more than they initially expected or they are unable to soothe their baby. Colic is a medical condition in which an otherwise healthy baby has frequent and extended periods of intense and unexplained crying and screaming. Colic tends to appear after the first month of life, and it disappears around the third or fourth month of life.

There are several causes of colic signs in babies—the most common of which include the following: stomach gas (due to poor burping), intestinal gas (pocketed in the intestinal tract), gastrointestinal reflux (silent, mild, and/or severe), neurological overload (overwhelmed, sleep deprived, and over-stimulated babies become exhausted and overtired, which prevents them from falling asleep, and makes them cry and fuss for hours), food allergies and complications (for example, lactose intolerance), and muscular pain (the baby who suffers from muscle spasms or the aftermath of birth trauma).

Sleep problems associated with colic tend to persist after the child has outgrown colic, simply because the strategies that parents put into place to decrease the crying episodes, such as holding and rocking the baby to sleep, strolling the baby to sleep, or consistently placing the baby on the bouncy seat or swing to sleep, interfere with the development of healthy sleep habits and positive sleep associations.

A baby who stops showing signs of colic during the day but who is still crying severely when put down to sleep, or who wakes up frequently during the night crying intensely but calms right away after being picked up when picked up, has most likely developed an unhealthy sleep pattern because.

With colicky babies, I still advise you to try and follow the Smooth Baby Sleep Approach as much as possible. When your child is crying, screaming, and fussing, you should do anything you need to do to help him feel better, calm down, and stop crying. However, that doesn't really mean that you have to continue doing those things until he is fully asleep; you can still try to place him to sleep on his back when he is drowsy, not crying, but awake. Even if only two out of ten times you manage to do that, you should keep trying. That way, once colic goes away, you will already have the habit of trying to get him in his crib before he falls asleep.

Acid Reflux

Gastroesophageal reflux disease (GERD) can be extremely painful and can cause colic, food resistance, weight loss, vomiting, iron deficiency, failure to thrive, irritability, and pulmonary disease, in the most severe cases. If your baby refuses feedings, takes very long to feed, arches her back while feeding (right after feeding or while trying to sleep), makes unusual noises while sleeping, sleeps in unusual positions, and/or spits ups or vomits often, you should consult with your pediatrician, because those are common signs of acid reflux.

I have personal experience dealing with this issue, since both of my daughters suffered from severe reflux, and they were both on reflux medication (Prevacid) for their first year of age. Despite that, they were (and still are) amazingly good sleepers, and they never developed an association between feeding and sleep or being held and sleep.

Therefore, my advice when dealing with babies with acid reflux is similar to the one I mentioned above for babies with colic. I still advise you to try and follow the Smooth Baby Sleep Approach as much as possible.

The common recommendations pediatricians give parents of a child suffering from reflux, besides giving him medication; are (1) to feed him less amounts, more often; (2) to burp their baby properly after every feeding, and (3) to hold him in an upright position for 20-40 minutes after every feeding. More often than not, babies do fall asleep during those 20 to 40 minutes, and they start associating you holding them with them falling asleep.

My recommendation is to design your child's schedule so that you feed him after sleep, or so that there's play time or awake time between feeding him and putting him to sleep. In the example below, you can see sample schedules of two, 4-month-old babies I worked with—one of them with reflux and one of them without reflux.

Time	Simon (GERD)	Alice (Not GERD)
6:00am	**Waking Time**	**Waking Time**
6:00am	*Nursing*	*Bottle*
6:30am		
8 am – 9am	Morning Nap	Morning Nap
9:00am		
9:30am	*Nursing*	
10:30am		*Bottle*
11:00am – 1pm	Mid-day Nap	Mid-day Nap
12:30pm	*Nursing*	*Bottle*
2:00pm		
2:30pm	*Nursing*	
3:00pm		
3:30pm – 4pm	Afternoon Nap	Afternoon Nap
4pm		
5:00pm	*Nursing*	Bath + Massage + Pajamas
5:00pm	Bath + Massage + Pajamas	*Bottle*
5:30pm	Bedtime	Bedtime
6pm-6am		
9:30pm	*Nursing*	
11:30pm		*Bottle*
2:00pm	*Nursing*	
Rest of Night		

Figure 22: GERD vs. Non-GERD 4-month-old baby schedules.

Note: White cells indicate times when the baby is playing and awake but not feeding.

Milk Allergy

Cow's milk is the most common allergen in infancy. The main symptoms among infants are: vomiting, diarrhea, abdominal cramps, abdominal bloating, skin rashes, blood in the stools, and/or respiratory symptoms, such as coughing and runny noses. Cow's milk allergy may cause difficulty falling asleep, disturbed sleep, frequent night wakings, shorter sleep cycles, and dramatic reductions in total sleep time.

Sleep Apnea

Childhood obstructive sleep apnea is a medical condition in which a child stops breathing in her sleep, which causes her to have partial wakings during the night, therefore preventing them from getting enough sleep. If the child doesn't wake up when she experiences the apnea or breathing difficulty, she may be at higher risk for Sudden Infant Death Syndrome (SIDS). Sleep apnea deprives children's brains of oxygen, which may cause more serious cognitive, health, and developmental problems.

The main symptoms of sleep apnea in children are the following:

- Loud and continuous snoring
- Failure to thrive
- Mouth breathing
- Enlarged tonsils and adenoids
- Restless sleep
- Constant night wakings
- Waking up tired

- Morning or night headaches
- Excessive daytime sleepiness
- Poor attention
- Hyperactivity
- Swelling of the legs
- Nocturia
- Nighttime choking or gasping spells
- Sweating and chest pain while sleeping
- Unusual sleeping positions
- Any unusual behavior

If you suspect that your child might have sleep apnea, talk to your pediatrician or a sleep specialist about it.

Teething

Teething is a natural, sequential process of growth of infant's teeth. The discomfort associated with teething can begin before any tooth appears. The main symptoms of teething are the following:

- Fussiness
- Excessive drooling
- Runny nose
- Rash on the chin or near the mouth
- Frequent biting and chewing on everything
- Red cheeks
- Refusing feeding
- Swollen gums
- High body temperature
- Earache not produced by ear infections
- Soft stools
- Diaper rash

Teething can start as early as three months and as late as twelve. This is the normal timetable for teeth to emerge:

- **6 to 12 Months**

  The lower incisor (the teeth at the very front of the mouth) is generally the first to emerge.

- **9 to 16 Months**

  Two more incisors break through—top and bottom.

- **12 to 18 Months**

  The first back molars emerge.

- **18 to 24 Months**

  The canine teeth start to appear between the molars and incisors.

- **24 to 40 Months**

  The second molars emerge.

Most babies don't have a full set of milk teeth (ten on the top and ten on the bottom) until around the age of three. They will then usually keep these until they are approximately six years of age. It is then that these will naturally start to fall out and are replaced by bigger, permanent teeth. Therefore, in my opinion, teething shouldn't interfere with sleep training, because your baby is going to be teething until she's about 3 years old. She needs to be able to sleep regardless of her teeth emerging.

Teething is more painful to some children than it is to others, so if you think it's being so painful to her that it's affecting her sleep, I'd definitely check with the pediatrician so that he can recommend something to help her alleviate that sensation a little bit. As a general rule, you can still sleep train your baby, even if she is teething, simply wait until the worse days are over.

Frequent Night Wakings

Night wakings are a normal part of adults and children's sleep patterns. What is not normal is for those wakings to last more than seconds or minutes and to become an interaction opportunity.

It's also very common, even for the best of sleepers, to start having sleep problems at some point during their childhood. When a baby/toddler over 3 months, with no health complications, and who doesn't have any of the sleep problems mentioned below, sets a pattern of waking up every 3 hours that means his body is conditioned to do so (habit). Therefore, regardless of the chosen sleep training method, consistency will be the key to solve his sleep problems.

These are some of the causes for these new sleep problems:

Sleep Deprivation

It may seem counterintuitive. However, the less sleep your child gets, the more likely he is to have trouble settling down at bedtime and staying asleep through the night.

Illness

One of the main causes of night wakings is illnesses—in particular, those that are painful and associated with a fever, such as ear infections. These frequent wakings often require your intervention to soothe your baby to fall back to sleep. This might be interiorized by your child, thinking that he needs you (holding, rocking, etc.) to fall asleep, even long after the illness is gone. It is a vicious cycle: illnesses disturb your children's sleep, and the lack of sleep makes them more vulnerable to illnesses.

Developmental Milestone/Leap

Many babies go through a phase of frequent night wakings, coinciding with a developmental change. For example, if she's just learned how to crawl, stand, or walk, she'll want to practice it every chance she gets, even when she wakes up in the middle of the night.

Teething

If you suspect teething at all, it may help to give your baby a pain reliever before bedtime (check with your baby's doctor for suggestions). Teething pain is often worse at night, but most kids sleep through it.

Room Temperature

Babies will wake up if they are too cold or too hot. This tends to happen during the winter (they are cold or overheated by their layers of clothing) and summer (they are too hot or too cold with the AC). Make sure your nursery is between 68-72 degrees F.

Night Terrors

Night terrors are often associated with sleep deprivation. When your child is having a night terror, she will cry hysterically, move, and seem confused, disoriented, and inconsolable. Trying to soothe your child will only extend and intensify the sleep terror. Don't try to vigorously awaken him. Let the night terror run its course, and stand nearby to make sure your child doesn't hurt himself.

Nightmares

Your child may also be having nightmares. Your child's imagination is developing, and that carries over into his sleeping world. Calm him and reassure him when this happens.

Night Weaning

A baby needs a certain amount of food every day. After the 6 months, most babies do not need any night feedings. If they don't get the right amount of food during the day, they'll ask for it at night. If you continue to nurse at night, they will continue not taking enough during the day. This too is a vicious cycle.

Sometimes, a child might feel hungry at night. However, that doesn't mean he can't go all night without a feeding; it simply means he needs to adjust how much he's eating during the day. The idea is to gently help him do this, while you're weaning him of his night feedings.

Many children (especially those who still have night feedings after the 9th month) crave those night nursing sessions—not because they're hungry or they need the calories, but because it's become a "social interaction" with mom.

The fastest transition tends to be "cold-turkey." Although this tends to be harder (emotionally) on the parents, it is usually the most effective one for babies over 9 months old.

It is advised to start following the new schedule for three to five days consistently, creating the routines, before night weaning. Once the new schedule is in place, pick a date for the night weaning and follow through with it.

Early Rising

Babies who wake up between 5:30am and 6:30am cheerful, happy, refreshed, and ready to start their day are in fact naturally early risers. A waking time in that range can be a biologically appropriate wake-up time for a child of this age. Therefore, when trying to shift their schedules, you're actually trying to re-program their bodies, which is not an easy task.

Without getting too far into technical talk about sleep, we all have internal clocks that drive when we wake and when we sleep. Shifting your child's schedule is adjusting this internal clock.

Most parents have a range of things they try when their children are getting up too early in the morning, such as:

- Putting their toddler to bed a bit later, hoping the extra tiredness will help him sleep longer;
- Increasing or decrease naptime hours during the day; and/or
- Bringing him in their bed in the morning.

While these options might work on a short-term basis, the truth is that the only long-term solution is having a good, tailored sleep schedule for your child. Putting in place sleep schedules and/or shifting them when necessary are the best way to improve the sleep habit of waking too early and going to bed too late.

Shifting Schedules

Early rising and schedule-shifting are, by far, the most challenging cases when it comes to sleep training, so please, be patient and consistent. Sometimes, it takes over 4 weeks to complete a full shift; sleep regressions are to be expected; and a few times, it is not possible to accomplish a full shift. It can be tough to get through, depending on how cranky your child gets, but it will be well worth it if you can stick to it.

It is very unlikely that you will have a shift of more than 0.5-1 hour at a time, and it is very unlikely that you will be able to generate a shift of more than 1.5 hours total.

There is some intricacy to shifting schedules, and many parents make the critical mistake of only moving their child's bedtime to a later time—which does not work. You need to move your child's whole schedule, including feedings, naps, bedtime, play time, and bath time.

When dealing with an early riser, you can take advantage of a schedule shift that we all go through, and that's the daylight savings' spring ahead. If you're reading this book, your child is an early riser, and spring forward is about to happen, I'd invite you to continue reading this chapter for further information on schedule shifting.

Sleep Aids

I don't normally recommend external aids to help babies to sleep (white noise machines, sleeping sheep, music, etc.), as I mentioned in the Step One of the Smooth Baby Sleep Approach (Chapter Eight). However, when sleep training toddlers, especially those with early rising habits, I would suggest introducing a "Sleep Clock." These aren't as effective for babies as they are for toddlers, but when your child is a naturally early riser, it's never too early to start using these sleep helpers.

You will set your child's waking time on the sleep clock, at which time a picture or image changes, a light comes on, or something happens indicating to your child that it is an appropriate time to wake up. Some sleep clocks have some other features, like playing a song at the waking time, and the ability to be an alarm clock, a night-light, or a game.

Make it a rule that she can't get out of bed until the sleep clock says it's time to start the day. At that time, she can call for you, and mommy or daddy will come get her.

I would also recommend that you set up a sticker chart and reward her when she stays in bed, quietly, until waking time. After so many stickers, she gets a small toy or prize or a one-on-one special date with mom or dad.

Nightmares & Night Terrors

Children spend more time dreaming than adults do, so they have more dreams—both good and bad. What is the difference between a nightmare and a night terror? Additionally, what should you do in each situation?

Nightmares are bad dreams that happen during rapid eye movement (REM) or dream sleep. Your child may be afraid to fall back asleep, and he'll probably remember that he had a bad dream. A baby or child who had a nightmare is likely to have a clear idea of what scared him, although he probably will not be able to vocalize his fright until he's about 2 years old.

The best responses to a **nightmare** are:

- Be there and offer comfort.
- Stay with your child until she feels relaxed and ready to sleep.
- Stay calm and convey to your child that what's happening is normal and that all is well.
- Reassure your child that she's safe and that it's OK to go back to sleep.
- If your child wakes with a nightmare, stay with her until she feels relaxed and ready to go to sleep.

The best way to prevent future nightmares is to help your child confront and overcome his fears of the dark, such as leaving a nightlight on or having a special stuffed toy to sleep with.

Night terrors occur in at least 5% of young children and can start as early as 9 months. These mysterious disturbances happen during deep, non-dreaming sleep. When a child is having a night terror, they will cry, whimper, flail, and even bolt out of bed.

Although his eyes may be wide open, he's not awake and isn't aware of your presence. Night terrors can last anywhere from a few minutes to half an hour, or more. Once it is over, your child will return to a sound sleep, and he will have no memory of the incident in the morning.

The best responses to **night terrors** are:

- Give him a gentle pat, along with comforting words or "shhh" sounds.
- Make sure he doesn't hurt himself.
- Don't speak to him, ask him questions, or try to hold or soothe him.
- Don't try to shake or startle him awake or physically restrain him—all of which could lead to more frantic behavior.

If it's a night terror, in 15 to 20 minutes, your child should calm down, curl up, and fall into a deep sleep again. If it's a nightmare, he might need a little more time to calm down and go back to sleep. To prevent night terrors, make sure that he is getting enough sleep, since children who go to bed overtired are more likely to experience these types of sleep disturbances.

Travel

Will travel ruin my baby's sleep habits? Will he/she be able to maintain the schedule? Should we maintain the schedule or just let him/her "run wild?" How do we adjust the schedules when there's a time difference? How do we handle his/her jet lag? Could you share some tips about baby and toddler sleep and travel?

These are only a few of the questions that we receive every year before summer, breaks, and holidays. In this section, I will address all those questions and share with you my tips for traveling with your baby.

Schedule & Timing

1. Schedule the in-flight or drive time to take place during a child's nap or bedtime.
2. Definitely keep your schedule (at local time)! You can move it 1-2 hours up or down, but you should maintain your routines and structure while on vacation. For example, if you're traveling to Southern Europe from the States, and your baby's schedule in the States is 6am to 6pm; you might be able to move him to 7am-7pm or even 8am to 8pm.
3. Do the naps! Do not think that skipping the nap will help your baby sleep better and faster at night. That's a common misconception. They will get to their bedtime overtired, and it will take them longer to fall asleep.
4. Feed your child at the usual mealtimes. Try to choose healthy, filling options; junk foods will only make the problem worse.

5. During naps and at night, make sure your baby's room is dark, and continue doing your naptime and bedtime routines.

6. Children (and adults) are conditioned to sleep when it is dark and to stay awake when it's bright light. However, our sleep-awake cycles are affected when we cross time zones. Children are more sensitive to light and dark cues than adults are, so use this to your advantage and to get rid of jet lag sooner. Wake up your child at the usual waking time, and expose him to day light as much as possible during the day (except for naps).

7. The first day at your destination, try to get as much sunlight as possible, as it will help your baby's body set into the new time zone easier and faster.

8. During the day, try to keep your child entertained and active. Exercise and play will wear him out and leave him ready for a good night's sleep.

Sleeping Environment & Routines

1. Arrange to have a full size crib wherever you are visiting (if your child still sleeps in a crib). If you cannot arrange to rent or borrow a crib, bring your own travel crib or pack and play. If you are taking a travel crib or pack and play, "rehearse" sleeping there at home for 2-3 days before you depart.

2. Spend some time bonding and playing with your child in the new room where she will be sleeping before bedtime or nap time.

3. Try to recreate your child's sleep environment. Bring familiar objects and sleeping props that you commonly use at home (i.e., sheets, certain books, loveys, white noise machines, pacifiers, etc.), and re-create her sleep environment.

4. If the room where your child will be sleeping does not have black-out shades, bring black garbage bags and painters' tape.

You can use them to darken the bedroom by taping them to the window.

5. Follow your child's normal sleep routines.

6. Do not introduce bad habits or poor sleep associations. Do not rock your baby to sleep, let him play longer than normal, let him sleep on your bed, let him watch TV before bedtime, etc. Do not create bad habits that you do not allow at home and that you will have to take away once your return.

7. If she wakes in the middle of the night crying for the first couple of nights, assume that she may acceptably be afraid. Help your child fall asleep using the closest method to what you do at home. However, if doesn't work, help her sleep any way you can, and don't worry too much about it. Every night will be better. If it's not, you'll need to retrain her back home.

8. Try to still do naps in her crib. If you need to do one nap out, pick the morning nap.

Everyone on Board!

More often than not, I hear from my clients that when they go visit grandma (nothing against grandmas!), their child's schedule gets completely derailed. Their child's sleep habits get worse, and they come back home with an overtired child, with new sleep routines. The best way to solve this type of problems is preventing them.

Let your hosts know about your schedule, sleeping routines, and the importance that getting a good night's sleep has to your child. Send them a copy of your child's schedule beforehand and mark the times when they can plan activities with your child, visits, and outings. Block the times where your baby will be napping or sleeping. Explain to them about your child's routines, and let them know if and how they can get involved.

228

This way, they know what to expect during your stay, and you will not run into unnecessary discussions. At the end of the day, the one suffering during these circumstances is your child, so let them know that these schedules and routines benefit your child.

Daylight Savings

Spring Forward

We "spring forward" to Daylight Savings Time (DST) on the second Sunday of March every year, until the first Sunday in November in the United States. This means that at 2:00am Standard Time, our clocks are moved forward by one hour, becoming 3:00am Daylight Savings Time (DST).

Baby sleep challenges are not uncommon during Daylight Savings Time adjustments. Still, the following are some general tips that you can follow to have a smoother transition, regardless of how you decide to adjust your child's schedule to the new time:

- Continue your bedtime and naptime routines. The regular and familiar routines you follow when putting your baby to sleep should be maintained.
- Keep your baby's nursery dark so that the daylight (and nightlight) changes do not interfere with his/her sleep.
- Carry on promoting positive sleep associations.
- Remember that consistency is still key.
- Change your watch and clocks to the new time before going to bed the day of the transition.

In addition to these measures, there are three basic approaches we can follow to help children with the transition that I will explain in detail below. Regardless of the approach you decide to take, remember that every child is different, and they will adjust differently to changes in their sleep schedule. It takes several days to adjust to the new times, so be prepared for your baby to want to wake up later than usual on occasions, to be crankier than usual during the afternoon, and/or to be sleepier during the first days of the transition. Be patient, loving, and consistent to ensure a smooth and successful transition.

Now, if your child is an **early riser**, you can take advantage of the DST change, and get him to sleep to a later time in the morning. So, if your child is waking up too early, don't do anything to adjust him to DST. Move his whole schedule one hour starting the day DST starts. For example, if your child usually wakes up at 5am and goes to bed at 5pm and that's too early for you; don't do anything after the time change, and her schedule will automatically become 6am to 6pm.

Gradual "Pre- Spring Forward Day" Transition

With this approach, you will prepare your child for the transition to the new time in advance. That transition will be progressive, so by the time Daylight Savings Time starts, your child will already be on his regular schedule on the new time.

Wednesday (4 Days Before Daylight Savings)

Wake up your child 15 minutes earlier from her last nap of the day. For example if her last nap of the day is usually from 12:30pm to 2:30pm, that Wednesday, she should sleep from 12:30pm (same time) to 2:15pm (you wake her up 15 minutes earlier than usual).

Make your child's bedtime 15 minutes earlier. For example, if your child's normal bedtime is 7pm. That Wednesday, she should go to sleep at 6:45pm—15 minutes earlier than usual.

Thursday (3 Days Before Daylight Savings)

On Thursday, move your child's daily schedule those 15 minutes. That means, you are going to wake up your child 15 minutes earlier than usual, in the morning, and her naps will start and finish 15 minutes earlier than usual.

Wake her up from her last nap of the day, another 15 minutes earlier. Continuing with the example above, if her last nap on Thursday should be from 12:15pm to 2:15pm (after moving those 15 minutes) wake her up at 2:00pm instead of 2:15pm (15 minutes earlier than you would).

Make your child's bedtime another 15 minutes earlier. Continuing with the example, her bedtime should be 6:45pm on Thursday, but instead it's going to be 6:30pm.

Friday and Saturday

Do the same thing you did Thursday. This way, you will have shifted your baby's schedule back by one hour by the time you have to move your clock forward one hour. Therefore, your baby would be in his normal schedule the first day of the Daylight Savings Time.

See the chart below for guidance. Note that this chart assumes baby's current bedtime is 7pm and waking time is 7am, with the first nap at 9am and the second one at 12:30pm.

Date	Transition Steps	Current Time (Standard Time)	New Time (Daylight Savings Time)
Wednesday	Wake up your baby from her last nap of the day 15 minutes earlier than usual. If she normally wakes up at 2:30pm, wake her up at 2:15pm.	2:15pm	3:15pm
	Move your baby's bedtime 15 minutes earlier (from your usual 7:00pm to 6:45pm).	6:45pm	7:45pm
Thursday	Move your baby's daily schedule those 15 minutes from the night before.	6:45am	7:45am
	Move your baby's bedtime another 15 minutes earlier.	6:30pm	7:30pm
Friday	Move your baby's daily schedule those 15 minutes earlier from the night before.	6:30am	7:30am
	Move your baby's bedtime another 15 minutes earlier.	6:15pm	7:15pm
Saturday (Spring Forward Night)	Move your baby's daily schedule those 15 minutes earlier from the night before.	6:15am	7:15am
	Move your baby's bedtime another 15 minutes earlier.	6:00pm	7:00pm
Sunday (1st Day in Daylight Savings)	Regular waking time 7:00am, under the new time (DST).	6:00am (Doesn't Apply)	**7:00am (New Time)**

Figure 23: Gradual "Pre-Spring Forward Day" Transition Example

For an even smoother transition, you can start moving your baby's bedtime 10 minutes earlier on Monday night instead of Wednesday.

Following this approach, you will help your child adjust to the new time, after the daylight savings time has started. The day after the daylight savings time starts, **Sunday**, your baby most likely would wake up one hour later than usual (based on the clock).

Sunday (First Day of Daylight Savings)

Wake her up 45 minutes later than her regular schedule. For example, if her regular waking time under standard time was 7am, with daylight savings time, that becomes 8am. However, you will not let her sleep until 8am. The first morning after the DST change, let her sleep only until 7:45am (45 later than her regular waking time).

From that moment on, make sure your child's naptime and bedtime that day are 45 minutes later than her regular schedule.

Monday

Wake her up 30 minutes later than her regular schedule. For example, if her regular waking time under standard time was 7am, with daylight savings time, that becomes 8am. However, you will not let her sleep until 8am. On the second morning after the DST change, let her sleep only until 7:30am (30 later than her regular waking time).

From that moment on, make sure your child's naptime and bedtime that day are 30 minutes later than her regular schedule.

Tuesday

Wake her up 15 minutes later than her regular schedule. For example, if her regular waking time under Standard Time was 7am, with Daylight Savings Time, that becomes 8am. However, you will not let her sleep until 8am. The second morning after the

234

DST change, let her sleep only until 7:15am (15 later than her regular waking time).

From that moment on, make sure your child's naptime and bedtime that day are 15 minutes later than her regular schedule.

Wednesday

Wake her up at her regular time. Continuing with the example above, you would wake her up at 7am. From this day on, she will be on her regular schedule, according to the Daylight Savings Time.

See the chart below for guidance. Note that this chart assumes baby's current bedtime is 7pm and waking time is 7am, with the first nap at 9am and the second one at 12:30pm.

Date	Transition Steps	Current Time (Standard Time)	New Time (Daylight Savings Time)
Sunday (Daylight Savings Time in Place since 2am)	Let your baby sleep 45 minutes over her regular waking time (7am in our example).	6:45am (Doesn't apply!)	7:45am
	Move your child's bedtime 45 minutes later than her regular bedtime (7pm in our example).	6:45pm	7:45pm
Monday	Let your baby sleep 30 minutes over her regular waking time (7am in our example).	6:30am	7:30am
	Move your child's bedtime 30 minutes later than her regular bedtime (7pm in our example).	6:30pm	7:30pm
Tuesday	Let your baby sleep 15 minutes over her regular waking time (7am in our example).	6:15am	7:15am
	Move your child's bedtime 15 minutes later than her regular bedtime (7pm in our example).	6:15pm	7:15pm
Wednesday	Wake your child up at her regular waking time (7am in our example). Continue the day with your child's regular schedule.	6:00am (Doesn't apply! Old Time)	7:00am

Figure 24: Gradual "Post-Spring Forward Day" Transition Example

236

The day after the daylight savings time starts, you follow your baby's regular schedule based on the Daylight Savings Time. Therefore, on Sunday, March 13, 2011, you switch your child "cold turkey" to the new time and follow her regular schedule.

You will most certainly have to wake your child up in the morning, since for her, it'd be one hour too early, and go on with her day as usual. This option tends to be harder on children since (like adults) they would be "loosing" one hour of sleep the first day.

Fall Back

We "fall back" to Standard Time on the first Sunday of November at 2am by setting our clock back one hour—so 2am becomes 1am. For adults that usually sounds great, as we have one extra hour of sleep at night. However, that usually means that our children will wake up one hour earlier the following morning.

Baby sleep challenges are not uncommon during daylight savings time adjustments. Still, there are some general tips that you can follow to have a smoother transition, regardless of how you decide to adjust your child's schedule to the new time:

- Continue your bedtime and naptime routines. The regular and familiar routines you follow when putting your baby to sleep should be maintained.
- Keep your baby's nursery dark so that the daylight (and nightlight) changes do not interfere with his/her sleep.
- Carry on promoting positive sleep associations.
- Remember that consistency is still key.

- Change your watch and clocks to the new time before going to bed.

In addition to these measures, there are three basic approaches we can follow to help children with the transition that I will explain in detail below. Regardless of the approach you decide to take, remember that every child is different and that they will adjust differently to changes in their sleep schedule.

It takes several days to adjust to the new times, so be prepared for your baby to want to wake up later than usual on occasions, to be crankier than usual during the afternoon, and/or to be sleepier during the first days of the transition. Be patient, loving, and consistent to ensure a smooth and successful transition.

‿ Gradual "Pre-Fall Back Day" Transition

With this approach, you will prepare your child for the transition to the new time in advance. That transition will be progressive, so by the time Standard Time is restablished, your child will already be on his regular schedule on the new time.

Wednesday (4 Days Before Standard Time)

Make your child's bedtime 15 minutes later. For example, if your child's normal bedtime is 7pm. That Wednesday, she should go to sleep at 7:15pm, 15 minutes later than usual.

Thursday (3 Days Before Standard Time)

On Thursday, move your child's daily schedule those 15 minutes. That means, you are going to wake up your child's 15 minutes later than usual, in the morning, and her naps will start and finish 15 minutes later than usual.

Wake her up from her last nap of the day, another 15 minutes later. Continuing with the example above, if her last nap on Thursday should be from 12:45pm to 2:45pm (after moving those 15 minutes) wake her up at 3pm instead of 2:45pm (15 minutes later than you would).

Make your child's bedtime another 15 minutes later. Continuing with the example, her bedtime should be 7:15pm on Thursday, but instead, it's going to be 7:30pm.

Friday and Saturday

Do the same thing you did Thursday. This way, you will have shifted your baby's schedule back by one hour by the time you have to move your clock backwards one hour. Therefore, your baby would be in his normal schedule the first day of the Standard Time.

See the chart below for guidance. Note that this chart assumes baby's current bedtime is 7pm and waking time is 7am, with the first nap at 9am and the second one at 12:30pm.

Date	Transition Steps	Current Time (Daylight Savings Time)	New Time (Standard Time)
Wednesday	Move your baby's bedtime to 7:15pm.	**7:15pm**	6:15pm
Thursday	Move your baby's daily schedule, starting at wake-up time 7:15am.	**7:15am**	6:15am
	Move your baby's bedtime to 7:30pm.	**7:30pm**	6:30pm
Friday	Move your baby's daily schedule, starting at wake-up time 7:30am.	**7:30am**	6:30am
	Move your baby's bedtime to 7:45pm.	**7:45pm**	6:45pm
Saturday (Fall Back Night)	Move your baby's daily schedule, starting at wake-up time 7:45am.	**7:45am**	6:45am
	Move your baby's bedtime to 8:00pm	**8:00pm**	7:00pm
Sunday (Standard Time in Place)	Regular waking time 7:00am.	8:00am (Doesn't apply!)	**7:00am**

Figure 25: Gradual "Pre-Fall Back Day" Transition Example

For an even smoother transition, you can start moving your baby's bedtime 10 minutes later on Monday night instead of Wednesday.

240

The day after the daylight savings time ends, **Sunday**, your baby will most likely wake up one hour earlier than usual (based on the clock). Starting then, you should make sure your child's naptime and bedtime are 45 minutes earlier than her regular schedule the first day; 30 minutes earlier the second day; and 15 minutes earlier the third day.

The whole daily schedule adjusts to those changes accordingly. By doing this, your baby would be going to sleep and waking up at his regular times, based on the Standard Time, the Thursday after the Standard Time was reestablished.

See the chart below for guidance. Note that this chart assumes baby's current bedtime is 7pm and waking time is 7am, with the first nap at 9am and the second one at 12:30pm.

Date	Transition Steps	Current Time (Daylight Savings Time)	New Time (Standard Time)
Sunday (Standard Time in Place)	Your baby will wake up one hour earlier than usual (6:00am).	7:00am (Doesn't apply!)	6:00am
	Move up your baby's first nap time 45 minutes (8:15am, instead of 9:00am).	9:15am	8:15am
	Move up your baby's second nap time 45 minutes (11:45am, instead of 12:30pm).	12:45pm	11:45am
	Move up your baby's bedtime 45 minutes (6:15pm, instead of 7pm).	7:15pm	6:15pm

Day			
Monday	Your baby will wake up 45 minutes earlier than usual (6:15am).	7:15am (Doesn't apply!)	**6:15am**
	Move up your baby's first nap time 30 minutes (8:30am, instead of 9:00am).	9:30am	**8:30am**
	Move up your baby's second nap time 30 minutes (12:00pm, instead of 12:30pm).	1:00pm	**12:00pm**
	Move up your baby's bedtime 30 minutes (6:30pm, instead of 7pm).	7:30pm	**6:30pm**
Tuesday	Your baby will wake up 30 minutes earlier than usual (6:30am).	7:30am (Doesn't apply!)	**6:30am**
	Move up your baby's first nap time 15 minutes (8:45am, instead of 9:00am).	9:45am	**8:45am**
	Move up your baby's second nap time 15 minutes (12:15pm, instead of 12:30pm).	1:15pm	**12:15pm**
	Move up your baby's bedtime 15 minutes (6:45pm, instead of 7pm).	7:45pm	**6:45pm**
Wednesday	Your baby will wake up 15 minutes earlier than usual (6:45am).	7:45am (Doesn't apply!)	**6:45am**
	Move up your baby's first nap time to its usual time (9:00am).	10:00am	**9:00am**
	Move up your baby's second nap to its usual time (12:30pm).	1:30pm	**12:30pm**
	Move up your baby's bedtime to its usual time (7pm).	8:00pm	**7:00pm**
Thursday	Your baby will wake at his usual waking time.	8:00am	**7:00am**

Figure 26: Gradual "Post-Fall Back Day" Transition Example

For an even smoother transition, you can adjust your baby's schedule in increments of 10 minutes, so she'd be in her normal schedule the Saturday after the Standard Time is reestablished.

242

∾ *Immediate Transition*

The day after the Standard Time is reestablished, you would follow your baby's schedule based on Standard Time. You would switch your child "cold turkey" to the new time. This option tends to be harder on children and on parents, and would be only advisable for children who are extremely adaptable to changes and new schedules.

Chapter Ten

SPECIAL CONSIDERATIONS

"Exceptions are not always the proof of the old rule; they can also be the harbinger of a new one."

- MARIE VON EBNER-ESCHENBACH

Prematurity

If your baby was born prematurely, you already know that she has two ages: her chronological age and her adjusted age. Her **chronological age** is the number of days, weeks, and months since your baby was born. Her **adjusted age** is the age she would have had if she had been born in her due date. For example, if your baby is 12 weeks old and was born at 10 weeks premature, her adjusted age is her chronological age minus 10 weeks—therefore, she is 2 weeks old adjusted.

You can still follow the Smooth Baby Sleep Approach described in this book, but you need to use your child's adjusted age, instead of her real age (chronological) when following the guidelines. Therefore, **when you are designing your child's** optimal schedule or when you are choosing your sleep training method, make sure you use adjusted age and not real age.

Multiples - Twins, Triplets, and More

As a mother of twins myself, I know how challenging and frantic life becomes when dealing with more than one baby at a time. The general principles and guidelines that I explained throughout this book are applicable to multiples as well. However, there are two aspects of sleep training multiples that I would love to clarify:

1. Synchronization

I tend to recommend that parents keep their multiples as synchronized as possible. Once the right schedule is in place, synchronization is possible. Very rarely will your twins have completely opposite internal body clocks that will require you to have two different schedules in place. Most siblings are within the same range. The key is to remember to put them down to sleep at the same time for naps and nights.

Since your babies are the exact same age, their sleep needs are similar. Even if their individual sleep needs might be different, they will both be within the same range. If after tracking them both (individually) you realize that one of them needs to sleep a little bit longer than the other, you can let her sleep a little bit more for her naps. You might also need to let her sleep a little bit longer in the morning.

2. Separation

Many of the families with multiples that I work with ask me whether they should separate their children during the sleep training process. My answer is "No, you don't need to separate them. They will get used to each other's little noises, cries, and movements." It is not unusual to see one of your babies sleeping deeply, while the other one might be crying for you.

Having said that, if you think you are going to be more comfortable separating them, or if you have one twin who is a good sleeper and one who has more challenges, and you want to go through the process without bothering the good sleeper, go ahead and do so. However, I don't think that you need to do it. If you decide to separate them, you should take the better sleeper into another room, and leave the worse sleeper in the room where they will eventually sleep. Once the worse sleeper is sleeping well, you can bring the better sleeper back in.

Autistic Spectrum Disorders

Parents and caregivers of children on the autism spectrum know what it is like to be short of sleep. Sleep disorders are even more common among children with autism. In fact, studies estimate that between 40% and 80% of children with autism have sleep difficulties. Some researchers have suggested that the intensity of developmental disturbances and general autism symptoms is increased in relation to sleeping problems. Research has shown that there is a connection between lack of sleep and the following characteristics in children with autism:

- Aggression
- Depression
- Hyperactivity
- Increased behavioral problems
- Irritability
- Poor learning
- Cognitive performance

Sleep challenges may include, but are not limited to, the following:

- Difficulty settling in at night and falling asleep
- Difficulty staying asleep
- Frequent and long sleep awakening during the night
- Enuresis
- High variability or delay in sleep onset and wake times
- Inconsistent sleep routines
- Prolonged settling down routines
- Ritualistic behavior prior to bed
- Difficulty being alone in a room

- Abnormal activity pattern during the night
- Low sleep efficiency
- High sensitivity to light and sound
- Tactile defensiveness (to sheets, blankets, pajamas or covers)
- Daytime sleepiness
- REM sleep behavior disorder
- Periodic limb movements in sleep
- Obstructive sleep apnea
- Reduced sleep in the first two thirds of the night
- Insomnia
- Parasomnias (e.g., head banging, sleep terrors)
- Early morning rising

Every child's situation will be different and unique. However, researchers and medical professionals have the following several theories as to why autistic children have more problems with sleep than children out of the autistic spectrum:

1. Abnormal Melatonin Production

As I explained previously, the hormone melatonin helps regulate our sleep-wake cycles and our internal clock. Research has found some children with autism cannot release melatonin at the appropriate times of day—producing high levels of melatonin during the daytime and low levels during night—which makes them have unusual sleep-wake cycles and affects their sleep habits. Expose your child to sunlight as much as possible during the day to help him regulate his body's production of melatonin.

2. Hyper-sensitivity to External Stimuli

Children with autism tend to be more sensitive to external input, such as light, touch, and/or sound. If this is the case, a child with autism may wake up abruptly when his mother opens the bedroom door, walks in the hallway, dims the lights, uses the bathroom, or turns on the TV in another room.

3. Inability to Interpret Social Cues

Children use social cues (lower lights in the house, calmer atmosphere, getting a relaxing bath, and putting the pajamas on). Children with autism may misunderstand or fail to identify these cues.

Sleep Training Tips

Most of the aspects of the Smooth Baby Sleep Approach can also be applied to children with autism, with certain modifications. The main challenge, when it comes to sleep training children with autistic spectrum disorders, is to find the exact combination of external factors that will make his sleep better. Therefore, inevitably, the sleep training process of these children requires more trial and error than that of children out of the autistic spectrum.

Sleep training children in the autistic spectrum disorder can be extremely challenging, time-consuming, and frustrating at times. However, it is absolutely worth it. I have personally worked with several families with autistic children, and we have seen tremendous improvements in those children's sleep quality as long as the parents were consistent, had the right set of conditions and environment around their child's sleep, and had chosen the right sleep training approach for their child.

You need to be especially careful and vigilant when it comes to creating a soothing and safe sleep environment (see Chapter Eight – Step One), as children with autism tend to be more sensitive to external stimuli.

Temperature of the Room

Your child might be more sensitive than you to temperature changes. Pay close attention during the day, and try to figure out what temperature range makes him most comfortable.

Bedding, Sleep Clothes, and Loveys

Your child might be more sensitive to certain textures. Some textures might help him relax, while others might make him anxious and uncomfortable. Make sure your child's sheets, pajamas, and everything that is within touching distance is comfortable to him.

Your child might also prefer his feet uncovered or covered with socks, footed pajamas, sleep sacks, or sheets. Your child might also be sensitive to pressure, and he might have a preference around how tight or loose he wants his bedding.

Your child might also have a preference around the height of his mattress—some prefer to sleep on the floor, and some prefer to sleep at bed height. Your child might have a preference around the position of his crib or bed in the room—some kids want it to be in the center of the room with nothing touching or around the bed, and some want it in the corner. Your child might also have a preference around how big his sleeping space is—some children like to be confined to a small space, while others prefer having lots of room around them.

Sounds and Auditory Stimuli

Your child might be sensitive to noises around him while he is sleeping or trying to fall asleep. In over-sensitive children, the sightless sound might disturb their sleep. In these cases, I would recommend the use of a white noise machine, as it will help mask other noises.

Light and Visual Stimuli

Your child might need or prefer complete darkness to fall asleep, or he might be afraid of the dark and need some sort of night-light on—or anything in between.

❧ *Calming, Bonding, and Safe Sleep Rituals*

Establishing a firm routine appears to be essential helping autistic children develop positive sleep associations and healthy sleep habits.

A soothing and relaxing bedtime routine will help your child to slow down, relax, and get ready to sleep. When it comes to children with autistic spectrum disorders, you must not assume that what you find relaxing is necessarily going to be relaxing for your child. For instance, some autistic children might find their bath too stimulating, frightening, or upsetting. Therefore, incorporating baths into their bedtime routine will only make things worse. However, there might be other sensory activities that you know relax him that you can incorporate as part of the bedtime routine.

A new study published in the _Journal of Child Neurology_ has found that melatonin supplements might improve the sleep of children with autism. As a mother, I would rather try to help my child to sleep with a natural supplement, like melatonin, that is already in her body than to resort to other drugs to induce sleep. Especially, because in the case of children with autism, by giving them melatonin, you are giving them what their bodies are failing to produce in adequate amounts.

A few studies currently available do caution, however, that melatonin sometimes stops working and does not usually help those who frequently wake up during the night. In addition, the long-term effect of taking melatonin has not been established. Remember that I am not a physician. Always consult with your child's pediatrician before trying any supplements.

PART V:
APPENDIX

REFERENCE TABLES & GUIDELINES

Figure 1 and 7: Children's Sleep Needs by Age: Daytime and Nighttime Hours

Age	Sleep Needs		
	Day (Hours)	Night (Hours)	Total (Hours)
0 – 2 Month	5 – 7	10 – 13	15 – 18
3 – 4 Months	4 – 5	10 – 12	14 – 16
5 – 6 Months	4 – 5	10 – 12	14 – 16
7 – 9 Months	2 – 4	11 – 13	13 – 15
10 – 12 Months	2 – 4	11 – 13	13 – 15
3 – 14 Months	2 – 3	11 – 13	13 – 15
15 – 18 Months	2 – 3	11 – 13	13 – 15
19 – 24 Months	2 – 3	10 – 13	12 – 15
2 – 3 Years	1 – 3	10 – 12	11 – 14
3 – 5 Years	0 – 2	10 – 12	11 – 13
5 – 11 Years	0	9 – 12	9 – 12
12 – 17 Years	0	8 – 11	8 – 11

Note: The hours from each column don't always add up since children might take shorter naps and sleep more hours at night and vice versa.

Figure 2, 8 and 15: Daytime Children's Sleep Needs by Age: Naps and Hours

Age	Day (Hours)	Number of Naps
0 – 2 Month	5 – 7	Several
3 – 4 Months	4 – 5	4 – 3
5 – 6 Months	4 – 5	3 – 2
7 – 9 Months	2 – 4	2
10 – 12 Months	2 – 4	2
13 – 14 Months	2 – 3	2
15 – 18 Months	2 – 3	2 – 1
19 – 24 Months	2 – 3	1
2 – 3 Years	1 – 3	1
3 – 5 Years	0 – 2	1 – 0
5 – 11 Years	0	0
12 – 17 Years	0	0

Figure 3 and 10: Children's Sleep Needs by Age: "Sleeping Through the Night"

Age	Night Time Sleep	
	Night (Hours)	**Sleeping Through the Night:** Longest Stretch Without Waking (Number of Wakings)
0 – 2 Month	10 – 13	2.5 – 4 (many)
3 – 4 Months	10 – 12	4 – 8 (2 – 4)
5 – 6 Months	10 – 12	6 – 12 (0 –2)
7 – 9 Months	11 – 13	8 – 13 (0- 1)
10 – 12 Months	11 – 13	8 – 13 (0- 1)
13 – 14 Months	11 – 13	11 – 13
15 – 18 Months	11 – 13	11 – 13
19 – 24 Months	10 – 13	10 – 13
2 – 3 Years	10 – 12	10 – 12
3 – 5 Years	10 – 12	10 – 12
5 – 11 Years	9 – 12	9 – 12
12 – 17 Years	8 – 11	8 – 11

Figure 16: Naptime Scheduling Guidelines

Age	Morning Nap		Mid-Day Nap		Afternoon Nap	
	Gap*	Length	Gap*	Length	Gap*	Length
0 – 2 Month	Varies	Varies	Varies	Varies	Varies	Varies
3 – 4 Months	1.5 – 2	1 – 1.5	2 – 2.5	1 – 2.5	2 – 2.5	0.5 – 1
5 – 6 Months	2 – 2.5	1 – 1.5	2 – 2.5	1 – 2.5	2 – 2.5	0.5 – 1
7 – 9 Months	2 – 2.5	0.5 – 1.5	2.5 – 3	1.5 – 3	No Nap	
10 – 12 Months	2 – 3	0.5 – 1	2.5 – 3	1.5 – 3	No Nap	
13 – 14 Months	2 – 3	0.5 – 1*	2.5 – 5*	1 – 3	No Nap	
15 – 18 Months	No Nap		5 – 6	1.5 – 3	No Nap	
19 – 24 Months	No Nap		5 – 6	1.5 – 3	No Nap	
2 – 3 Years	No Nap		6 – 7	1 – 3	No Nap	
3 – 5 Years	No Nap		6 – 7*	1 – 2*	No Nap	
5 – 11 Years	No Nap		No Nap		No Nap	
12 – 17 Years	No Nap		No Nap		No Nap	

Figure 17: Bedtime Scheduling Guidelines

Age	Night Sleep		
	Night (Hours)	Bedtime (Hours from last Sleep)	Sleeping Through the Night - Longest Stretch Without Waking (# Wakings)
0 – 2 Month	10 – 13	Varies	2.5 – 4 (many)
3 – 4 Months	10 – 12	2 – 2.5	4 – 8 (2 – 4)
5 – 6 Months	10 – 12	2 – 3	6 – 12 (0 –2)
7 – 9 Months	11 – 13	3 – 5	8 – 13 (0- 1)
10 – 12 Months	11 – 13	3.5 – 5	8 – 13 (0- 1)
13 – 14 Months	11 – 13	4 – 5	11 – 13
15 – 18 Months	11 – 13	4 – 5	11 – 13
19 – 24 Months	10 – 13	4 – 5	10 – 13
2 – 3 Years	10 – 12	4 – 6	10 – 12
3 – 5 Years	10 – 12	11 – 14	10 – 12
5 – 11 Years	9 – 12	12 – 13	9 – 12
12 – 17 Years	8 – 11	13 – 16	8 – 11

Summary Table: Comprehensive Children's Sleep Needs by Age

Age	Day Sleep (Naps)								Night Sleep			TOTAL (Hours)
	Day (Hours)	Number Of Naps	Morning Nap		Mid-Day Nap		Afternoon Nap		Night (Hours)	Bedtime GAP[2]	Sleeping Through Night[3]	
			GAP[1]	Length	GAP[1]	Length	GAP[1]	Length				
0 – 2 Months	5 – 7	Several	Varies	Varies	Varies	Varies	Varies	Varies	10 – 13	Varies	2.5 – 4 (many)	15 – 18
3 – 4 Months	4 – 5	4 – 3	1.5 – 2	1 – 1.5	2 – 2.5	1 – 2.5	2 – 2.5	0.5 – 1	10 – 12	2 – 2.5	4 – 8 (2 – 4)	14 – 16
5 – 6 Months	4 – 5	3 – 2	2 – 2.5	1 – 1.5	2 – 2.5	1 – 2.5	2 – 2.5	0.5 – 1	10 – 12	2 – 3	6 – 12 (0 – 2)	14 – 16
7 – 9 Months	2 – 4	2	2 – 2.5	0.5 – 1.5	2.5 – 3	1.5 – 3	No Nap		11 – 13	3 – 5	8 – 13 (0 – 1)	13 – 15
10 – 12 Months	2 – 4	2	2 – 3	0.5 – 1	2.5 – 3	1.5 – 3	No Nap		11 – 13	3.5 – 5	8 – 13 (0 – 1)	13 – 15
13 – 14 Months	2 – 3	2	2 – 3	0.5 – 1	2.5 – 5	1 – 3	No Nap		11 – 13	4 – 5	11 – 13	13 – 15
15 – 18 Months	2 – 3	2 – 1	No Nap		5 – 6	1.5 – 3	No Nap		11 – 13	4 – 5	11 – 13	13 – 15
19 – 24 Months	2 – 3	1	No Nap		5 – 6	1.5 – 3	No Nap		10 – 13	4 – 5	10 – 13	12 – 15
2 – 3 Years	1 – 3	1	No Nap		6 – 7	1 – 3	No Nap		10 – 12	4 – 6	10 – 12	11 – 14
3 – 5 Years	0 – 2	0 – 1	No Nap		6 – 7	1 – 2	No Nap		10 – 12	11 – 14	10 – 12	11 – 13
5 – 11 Years	0	0	No Nap		No Nap		No Nap		9 – 12	12 – 13	9 – 12	9 – 12
12 – 17 Years	0	0	No Nap		No Nap		No Nap		8 – 11	13 – 16	8 – 11	8 – 11

¹ *GAP*: refers to the time that should pass between the last time your child woke up and the beginning of the following sleep period. For example, when we are referring to the morning nap, this GAP is the hours between his natural waking time and the ideal time for his morning nap to start. When we are talking about the mid-day nap this GAP is the hours between the end of his morning nap and the ideal time for his mid-day nap to start, if your child still has a morning nap. If your child doesn't have a morning nap, this GAP is the hours between his natural waking time and the ideal time for his mid-day nap to start.

² *Bedtime GAP:* refers to the time that should pass between the end of your child's last nap and his bedtime.

³ *Sleeping Through the Night:* refers to the longest stretch that your child could go without waking up. In parenthesis you will see the number of wakings that are considered average for a child that age.

Figure 18: Feeding Guidelines

AGE	WHAT?	DAY		NIGHT	
		Freq.	Number	Freq.	Num.
0 – 1 Months	Breast milk OR Formula	2 – 4	4 – 6	2 – 4	4 – 6
1 – 2 Month	Breast milk OR Formula	3 – 4	4 – 5	3 – 4	4 – 5
3 – 4 Months	Breast milk OR Formula	4	4	4 – 8	4 – 2
5 – 6 Months	Breast milk OR Formula	4	4	6 – 12	0 – 2
6 – 8 Months	Breast milk OR Formula	4	4		
	Solids (Cereal, Fruits, Veggies)	2 – 4	3		
9 – 12 Months	Breast milk OR Formula	4	4		
	Solids (Add protein + Finger Foods)	2 – 4	3 + 2 Snacks		
13 – 18 Months	Breast Milk OR Whole Milk	2 - 4	3		
	Solids (Add nuts)	2 – 4	3 + 2 Snacks		
19 – 24 Months	Breast Milk OR Whole Milk	2 - 4	3		
	Solids	2 – 4	3 + 2 Snacks		
25 – 36 Months	Breast Milk OR 2% Milk	2 - 4	3		
	Solids	2 – 4	3 + 2 Snacks		

Figure 20: Regular Comfort & Reassurance Intervals (In Minutes)

Age	1st Check In	2nd Check In	3rd Check In & Following
Children 6 to 12 Months of Age	3	6	12
Children 13 to 18 Months of Age	4	7	15
Children 19 Months and Older	5	8	18

TEMPLATES & TRACKERS

Template 1: Daily Log (Figure 4, 5 and 6)

Time	Sleep	Mood	Feeding	Diapering/ Potty	Activity	Other Comments
6:00am						
6:30am						
7:00am						
7:30am						
8:00am						
8:30am						
9:00am						
9:30am						
10:00am						
10:30am						
11:00am						
11:30am						
12:00pm						
12:30pm						
1:00pm						
1:30pm						
2:00pm						
2:30pm						
3:00pm						
3:30pm						
4:00pm						
4:30pm						
5:00pm						
5:30pm						
6:00pm						
6:30pm						
7:00pm						
7:30pm						
8:00pm						
8:30pm						

Time	Sleep	Mood	Feeding	Diapering/ Potty	Activity	Other Comments
9:00pm						
9:30pm						
10:00pm						
10:30pm						
11:00pm						
11:30pm						
12:00am						
12:30am						
1:00am						
1:30am						
2:00am						
2:30am						
3:00am						
3:30am						
4:00am						
4:30am						
5:00am						
5:30am						

Template 2: Comprehensive Daytime Sleep Assessment (Figure 9, 11 and 13)

Days	Day (Hours)	Number of Naps	Morning Nap				Mid-Day Nap				Afternoon Nap			
			Hours since last sleep (waking)	Nap's Length	# Wakings	Wakings' Duration (Minutes)	Hours since last sleep (morning nap or waking*)	Nap's Length	# Wakings	Wakings' Duration (Minutes)	Hours since last sleep (mid-day nap or waking)	Nap's Length	# Wakings	Wakings' Duration (Minutes)
Day 1														
Day 2														
Day 3														
Day 4														
Day 5														
Average														
Sleep Needs*														
GAP														
Conclusions														

264

Template 3: Comprehensive Nighttime Sleep Assessment (Figure 12 and 14)

Days	Night Sleep				
	Hours since last sleep (last nap)	Longest stretch without waking	Night Wakings		
			Number	Duration of Wakings in Minutes	Total Awake Time
Day 1					
Day 2					
Day 3					
Day 4					
Day 5					
Average					
Sleep Needs*					
GAP					
Conclusions					

* From Comprehensive Children's Sleep Needs By Age table seen above.

Template 4: Smooth Baby Sleep Plan

Current Situation
<Brief Description of Your Child's Main Sleep Challenges>

Desired Situation: Right Expectations & Goals
<Write down your quantitative and qualitative sleep training goals>

Appropriate Attitude & Mindset

- Be calm, patient, and nurturing.

- Be open-minded and willing.

- Be consistent.

- Make sleep a priority.

- Don't expect miracles.

Calming, Bonding, and Safe Sleep Rituals

< Write down the tips and suggestions that you are going to implement, out of all those explained in chapter eight>

Safe and Soothing Sleep Haven

<Write down the changes/ improvements you need to put in place, based on what you learned on chapter eight – step one>

Everyone on Board

<List all the people who currently take care of your child on occasions and during her naps and/or bedtime>

Starting Date
<Write down the date>

Schedule
<Write down the schedule that you've just designed for your child>

Sleep Coaching Method
<Write down the name and steps of the sleep coaching method that you've decided to follow>

Breakdown of Responsibilities

	Morning Nap	Mid-day Nap	Bedtime	Night Wakings
Day 1				
Day 2				
Day 3				
Day 4				
Day 5				
Day 6				
Day 7				
Day 8				
Day 9				
Day 10				
Day 11				
Day 12				
Day 13				
Day 14				
Day 15				

WORKS CITED, SOURCES & BIBLIOGRAPHY

Consulted Websites

- National Sleep Foundation – www.sleepfoundation.org
- American Academy of Pediatrics – www.aap.org
- www.aboutourkids.org
- www.healthychildren.org
- www.parentingscience.com
- www.psych.nyu.edu
- www.end-your-sleep-deprivation.com
- www.drgreene.com
- www.webmd.com

Consulted Articles & Research

- Seminars in Pediatric Neurology, March 1996
- Journal of Pediatric Psychology, June 1997
- Pediatrics, December 1987
- "Are Your Students Sleep Deprived?" Education World. Education World. 10 May 2004.
- "Even Kids Suffer from Sleep Deprivation." CNN.com. 5 May 2004.
- "Grade Schoolers Grow into Sleep Loss." Science News. Science News, May 20, 2000, by B. Bower. 5 May 2004.
- "Lack of Sleep Takes Toll on Brain Power." WebMDHealth.

- "Sleep Deprivation." My Healthy Advantage Children's Health. LifeWise Health Plan of Oregon. 5 May 2004.
- "Sleep Deprivation and ADHD." Dr. Greene, 5 May 2004.
- "Study Links TV Viewing to Sleep Deprivation in Children." The Daily Ardmoreite. 5 May 2004.
- "Clinical Manual for the Treatment of Autism" by Hollander E., Anagnostou E. American Psychiatric Publishing, Inc. 2007.
- "Handbook of Autism and Pervasive Developmental Disorders." 4th Edition, Volumes 1 & 2. John Wiley & Sons, Inc. 2005.
- "The Research Basis for Autism Intervention" by Arebell S, Ben-Zion I. "Sleep Problems in Autism." In: Schopler, E., Yirmiya, N., Schulman, C., Marcus, L.M. Kluwer Academic and Plenum Publishers.
- "Sleep in Children with Autism and Asperger Syndrome" by Richdale, A.
- "Sleep Disturbance in Children and Adolescents with Disorders of Development: Its Significance and Management." Mac Keith Press; 2001.
- "A Clinical Guide to Pediatric Sleep: Diagnosis and Management of Sleep Problems" by Mindell, J.A., Owens, J.A. Lippincott Williams & Wilkins; 2003.
- "Differential Diagnosis of Pediatric Sleep Disorders" by Sheldon, S.H., Ferber, R., Kryger, M.H. Principles and Practice of Pediatric Sleep Medicine.
- "Autistic Disturbances of Affective Contact" by Kanner, L.

Books Consulted

- *The American Academy of Pediatrics, Caring for Your Baby: Birth to Age Five.* Steven P. Shelov, M.D., F.A.A.P.

EXCLUSIVE

$30

GIFT CERTIFICATE

~Only for 'SMOOTH BABY SLEEP' readers~

To redeem:

- Visit our website **www.SmoothParenting.com**
- Call us at **646.450.6605**

Disclaimer and redemption rules: This gift certificate is transferrable and must be applied to Sleep Consultations and Parenting Coaching Services. It cannot be applied towards the purchase of online classes, mobile applications, books, CDs or DVDs, or services with a value equal to or less than $200.

Made in the USA
San Bernardino, CA
24 November 2013